W9-ASQ-226

UWM BOOKSTORE

$ X 5 2 0

USED-KEY II

H82

PSYCHOLOGICAL RESEARCH

AN INTRODUCTION

UWM BOOKSTORE

$X5.50

USED-KEY.R

PSYCHOLOGICAL
RESEARCH

AN INTRODUCTION
FOURTH EDITION

Arthur J. Bachrach
Naval Medical Research Institute

RANDOM HOUSE

NEW YORK

Fourth Edition

987654321

Copyright © 1962, 1965, 1972, 1981 by Random House, Inc.

All rights reserved under International and Pan-American Copyright
Conventions. No part of this book may be reproduced in any form
or by any means, electronic or mechanical, including photocopying,
without permission in writing from the publisher. All inquiries should
be addressed to Random House, Inc., 201 East 50th Street, New
York, N.Y., 10022. Published in the United States by Random
House, Inc., and simultaneously in Canada by Random House of
Canada Limited, Toronto.

Library of Congress Cataloging in Publication Data

Bachrach, Arthur J
    Psychological research.

    Bibliography: p. 185
    Includes index.
    1. Psychological research.   I. Title.
[DNLM: 1. Psychology 2. Research BF76.5
B124p]
BF76.5.B3   1980   150'.72   80-22842

ISBN: 0-394-32288-6

Text design by Barbara Sturman

Cover design by Jurek Wajdowicz

Manufactured in the United States of America

DEDICATION

For Susan,

and for John and Hunter

Preface

Many years ago, a writer who went solely by the initials K.M.S. observed that a preface is very much like a front tooth—it is never noticed unless it's missing. Using another metaphor, K.M.S. also noted that a preface is similar to a dandelion over which a lawnmower skips quickly, presumably as a reader quickly skips over a preface, over material that does not belong to the main body of the book.

If, indeed, this is the way prefaces are viewed (and I have no reason to believe that they are not) the author would find this unfortunate because it is the appropriate forum for the expression of gratitude to those who have helped in the creation of the book. For this, the fourth edition, it is particularly important to me to recognize those students who, over the years, have been interested enough to write and express their thoughts about the book, thoughts that have been, in many cases, incorporated into revisions. I hope to have more comments so that I may consider them for the next edition and have an augmented fifth.

The support of the Naval Medical community in my research is gratefully acknowledged. I should like to add, however, that the opinions expressed in this book are my own and do not necessarily reflect those of the Naval Service.

In past editions I have had the delightful opportunity to thank friends and associates who contributed to the work. For this edition, the excellent editorial team at Random House—Virginia Hoitsma, Stephen Deitmer, and James Kwalwasser—provided much valued support and advice. I am particularly grateful to another editorial team whose interest, support, warmth, and expertise contributed importantly to the formulation of ideas and their presentation—my two close friends and colleagues, Mary Margaret Matzen and Doris Auer.

Contents

1

Some Important Characteristics of Science and Scientists

Research is *not* statistics. I am beginning this introduction to psychological research with this negative statement because I feel that many students are scared away from the enjoyable pursuit of research because they equate it with tedium and involved statistical manipulations. This misapprehension is not difficult to understand, for a student who picks up a typical book on research is likely to find it no more than a text on statistics in research design. My intent is not to disparage statistics in any way, but merely to indicate that it is a *tool* of research—a useful one, to be sure, but no more than a technique for handling some (not all) research data.

Just as research is not statistics, science is not technology. The development of a new camera, for example, is a scientific proposition drawing upon the knowledge and technical data available to educated researchers, but it is not science in its larger sense. Science in that sense is a means of acquiring information, of searching more or less systematically for answers, for discoveries of new relationships. Science as technology can produce objects to make our daily lives easier (or more difficult, depending on how you view an object such as television).

A large part of this problem of perception is that the social sciences have not kept up technologically with the physical sciences and engineering. As an example, we are aware that modern technologies of "aqua-culture" fish farming could (and probably will) provide needed protein for the world's population; but social scientists lag behind this existing technology in not being able to provide answers as to how large segments of critical populations—in India or our own Southwest, for example—can be introduced to a diet that, although nutritionally important and inexpensive, is foreign to their lifestyle. On a more philosophical scale, value systems seem to fall behind technology. As Einstein once said, "A perfection of means and a confusion of aims, seems to be our main problem."

Science as a means of acquiring information combines, as Albert Szent-Györgyi once said, curiosity and human creativity (138).* But knowledge and wisdom have to be distinguished from each other. The philosopher Alfred North Whitehead once said that knowledge is more perishable than fresh fish. The important aspect of science-as-means is that it focuses upon discovering facts that change as more information is acquired. This is the basis of what is referred to loosely as "the scientific method" and will be a major focus of this little volume.

It is also true that books on research tend to be formalized statements of principles and methods necessarily presented as distilled ideals. To use an analogy, a research book is formal like a tuxedo while research activity is informal like working blue-jeans. At this time I will state my First Law: "People don't usually do research the way people who write books about research say that people do research"; and my Second Law: "Things take more time than they do."

I am going to deal with research from a standpoint different from the traditional one, briefly mentioning some of its basic features (such as control and experimental groups), but not making any attempt to introduce the student to statistical techniques.

---

* Numbers in parentheses refer to numbered entries in the references at the back of the book.

Rather, my concerns are the origins of research, scientific method and practice, the meaning of data and theory, the ethical aspects of research with animal and human subjects, and, most important, the curiosity of scientists—their main attribute and source of pleasure. As the brilliant chemist Linus Pauling once observed, "Satisfaction of one's curiosity is one of the greatest sources of happiness in life."

Curiosity, Accident, and Discovery

> "A discovery is said to be an accident meeting a prepared mind."
> —Albert Szent-Györgyi

Let us start with the curiosity of the scientist. Much research begins with accidental discovery. A scientist is working diligently in his laboratory with a particular problem and a particular goal in view when something happens, perhaps goes wrong. Sir Alexander Fleming, whose findings led to the discovery of penicillin, had this happen when he was trying to culture some bacteria. You will recall that a little green mold was present in a dish in which he was culturing bacteria, and that the bacteria had been destroyed. This had probably happened to many scientists before him who might have sworn under their breaths about the ruined experiment, tossed the culture into the refuse, and started over again.

But this would have been contrary to scientific method in its ideal form. At its simplest, after a problem has been selected the scientific method consists fundamentally of two parts: (1) the collection of data and (2) the establishment of a functional relationship among these data.* For Fleming and those before him there were two coexisting basic data: (A) A bacteria culture was destroyed, and (B) a green mold was present in the dish.

---

* I am using "functional" in the sense in which it is used in the physical sciences, that the behavior of one event is related to the behavior of another event.

Now, was there a functional relationship between these two? Did A have any effect on B? This was the beginning of the research—to manipulate the conditions under which A and B coexisted so that an answer might be obtained. If they were functionally related (that is, A had an effect on B) that would be one answer; if they were not related and the coexistence was pure chance, that would also be an answer.

So Fleming started with an *observation*. He then planned an *experiment*—a controlled testing of a *hypothesis* based on observation. To start his experiment he probably formulated some sort of hypothesis which he probably stated roughly as follows: "The appearance of the green mold and the destruction of the colony of bacteria are related; the green mold was responsible for the destruction of the bacteria." From this point he proceeded to test his hypothesis. One approach would have been to take the green mold and put a new colony of live bacteria in contact with it. The results would have either confirmed or refuted the hypothesis. If the second colony of bacteria had also perished when in contact with the green mold, then the experimenter might have felt more comfortable in assuming a causal relationship. There are other factors to be taken into consideration, of couse, such as temperature changes and the presence or absence of sunlight. But assuming for the moment that these factors have been controlled, the experiment was to manipulate the green mold and bacteria under various controlled conditions.

Of course, Fleming's research showed that the mold was responsible for the bacterial destruction, and penicillin emerged from his findings. I want to emphasize the most important aspect of this: Fleming discovered this green mold by *accident;* he had merely been attempting to culture a particular colony of bacteria. A lesser man might have been irritated and annoyed at the death of the bacteria and might have ignored the mold and washed the entire dish down the sink. That Fleming did not do this illustrates one of the characteristics of a good scientist: He has his eyes open; he is never so bound up in a fixed path of experimentation that he is blinded to unusual events that may occur.

There were other ways in which accident played a role in Fleming's discovery.* Fleming's laboratory was a modest one; had he been able to work in a more controlled and protected environment, the contamination would not have occurred. He was also fortunate in that he was working with staphylococci, which happen to be particularly sensitive to penicillin's antibiotic action. And Fleming was sensitized to such a discovery because he had devoted years of research to finding a bactericidal agent with maximal effectiveness and minimal toxicity to human biology.

Other factors intervened. The initial response to Fleming's paper, published in 1929 (64), was almost exclusively by bacteriologists and biochemists. Physicians, on the other hand, were enthused by advances in chemical treatments then in process; the sulfanilamides (sulphur derivatives) were showing enormous promise as antibacterials. In addition, the purity of the antibiotics of the sort discovered by Fleming had not yet been achieved, and they were somewhat unstable. However, René Dubós's work in directing microorganisms against other microorganisms as an antibacterial therapy opened up new possibilities and interest.

At this time the so-called "Oxford Team" in England, led by such investigators as Chain, a chemist, and Florey, a pathologist, began large-scale research into the antibacterial use of penicillin. Their results were excellent; but here again chance played a role. Fully to pursue penicillin and its potential required a laboratory and a group of scientific personnel far greater than the Oxford Team possessed. Florey's first real experimental breakthroughs came in the summer of 1941, when the world was at war and the need for effective antibiotics had become acute. Florey and his associate Heatley were brought to the United States and given resources far beyond any they could have otherwise assembled. The cooperation of universities, laboratories, and pharmaceutical firms allowed these

---

* For a detailed analysis of this and other interesting scientific discoveries involving accidents, see Taton (139).

talented investigators to bring the development of penicillin to a successful conclusion. In 1945 Fleming, Chain, and Florey were awarded the Nobel Prize in Physiology/Medicine for their work.

Thus, chance and talent prevailed.

Ways Scientists Work—Sometimes

B. F. Skinner in one of his "unformalized principles of science" says, "When you run onto something interesting, drop everything else and study it" (123). While this may not fit the image of science and the scientist that the student has conceived, it does illustrate the way much research originates and develops. To the outsider looking at science, it often seems a logical, consistent, highly organized body of information revolving around a hard core of rigid, specified methodology. However, J. Z. Young in his treatise on science had the following to say:

> One of the characteristics of scientists and their work, curiously enough, is a confusion, almost a muddle. This may seem strange if you have come to think of science with a big S as being all clearness and light. There is indeed a most important sense in which science stands for law and certainty. Scientific laws are the basis of the staggering achievements of technology that have changed the Western world, making it, in spite of all its dangers, a more comfortable and a happier place. But if you talk to a scientist you may soon find that his ideas are not all well ordered. He loves discussion, but he does not think always with complete, consistent schemes, such as are used by philosophers, lawyers, or clergymen. Moreover, in his laboratory he does not spend much of his time thinking about scientific laws at all. He is busy with other things, trying to get some piece of apparatus to work, finding a way of measuring something more exactly, or making dissections that will show the parts of an animal or plant more clearly. You may feel that he hardly knows himself what law he is trying to prove. He is continu-

ally observing, but his work is a feeling out into the dark, as it were. When pressed to say what he is doing he may present a picture of uncertainty or doubt, even of actual confusion. (152)

Although the methodology of the scientist may appear haphazard, there is an overall conception of the goals. Excursions into such areas as apparatus design, freewheeling discussion, and other enjoyable side-paths nevertheless remain within the ultimate plan of knowledge and its discovery.

There are times when the curiosity of the scientist is piqued by the unusual and the unexplained in situations that do not lend themselves easily to experimentation but are potential stimuli to research. Let me give you an example of one such curious situation. Some time ago a famous world traveler gave the following description of the planet Mars and its satellites:

> They have . . . discovered two lesser stars or satellites which revolve around Mars whereof the innermost is distant from the center of the primary planet exactly three of his diameters and the outermost five; the former revolves in the space of ten hours, and the latter in twenty-one and a half; so that the squares of their periodical times are very near in the same proportion with the cubes of their distance from the center of Mars, which evidently shows them to be governed by the same law of gravitation that influences the other heavenly bodies. (69)

This is an accurate picture of Mars. It does have two moons, and the given revolutions are quite close to the actual periods. Phobos goes around Mars in the same direction in which the planet rotates, but in about one-third the time; this makes it appear to rise in the West and set in the East. It has been noted that this is the only known body in the universe that revolves around a central body faster than the central body rotates. Despite the fact that this is unique, it is in the traveler's description, and we find that it is a most accurate portrayal of Mars and the unusual nature of its satellites.

Why should this be so interesting? Because the famous "world traveler" who wrote this was Lemuel Gulliver as depicted by Jonathan Swift in 1726 in *Gulliver's Travels,* and the two moons were not discovered until 1877, a century and a half after Gulliver's description. As a matter of fact, no telescope big enough to see the moons was built until about 1820.

This is one way research begins: "How come?" While this may sound too colloquial for the scientific mind, it expresses the beginning of wonderment. How was Swift able to describe these moons so accurately 150 years before they were discovered? Is it coincidence? Is it possible that he had some information that others did not have? Was it merely a good guess? We have no answer to this, but it does provide stimulation for possible investigation.

The Prepared Mind

The mathematician George Polya once wrote, "The first rule of discovery is to have brains and good luck" (106). George Nelson tells of a similar comment by Pasteur:

> At a big reception at which Pasteur was the guest of honor one of his colleagues came up and said, "Isn't it extraordinary these days how many scientific achievements of our century are arrived at by accident?" Pasteur said, "Yes, it really is remarkable when you think about it, and furthermore, did you ever observe to whom the accidents happen?" (99)

Pasteur's answer stemmed from his avowed belief that "chance favors only the prepared mind." Certainly, this quality is foremost among those a good researcher needs. It is clearly impossible for anyone engaged in research to predict all of the events that may occur. The researcher must begin with care in the planning and execution of the research, but must not become so rigidly tied to the plan as to be rendered incapable of seeing accidental discoveries that may pop up. The researcher should approach this much in the way Fleming did in the example given above regarding the accidental discovery of penicillin. The researcher must be a little casual, in fact, for a relaxed but nevertheless alert view toward research may provide the occasion for unexpected or chance discovery. This is what Pasteur means by the "prepared mind"—a combination of stored basic knowledge and a readiness to perceive the unusual.*

Walter B. Cannon in his work *The Way of an Investigator* has referred to this type of accidental discovery as "serendipity" (44). This is a term taken from Walpole's *Three Princes of Serendip,* the story of three princes who went around the world searching for something, did not find what they were seeking, but on their journeys discovered many things that they had not sought. Cannon indicates that serendipity—accidental discovery— is a major quality of research and the prepared mind must be alert for it.

A Case of Serendipity

In a research report designed specifically to study examples of accidental discovery and the ways of an investigator, two sociologists, Bernard Barber and Renée Fox, interviewed two well-qualified research scientists, both of whom had observed an event while only one had followed through to an eventual discovery. Barber and Fox call this article "The Case of the Floppy-Eared Rabbits: An Instance of Serendipity Gained and Serendipity Lost" (18). Because this is one of the most valuable examples available of accidental discovery, I would like to discuss it in some detail.

---

* There is charming irony about this. In 1877, about fifty years before Fleming's discovery of penicillin, Pasteur and his colleague Joubert observed the same event while culturing a colony of anthrax bacilli and found that airborne microorganisms impeded the development of the culture. Recognizing the potential importance of this finding, they conducted one simple experiment, but then dropped the research, because of the many other problems on which they were working. The "prepared mind" was otherwise absorbed.

Barber and Fox had heard of a discovery two researchers had made accidentally. One of these two scientists was Dr. Lewis Thomas, an eminent scientist who at the time of the paper (1958) was head of the Department of Medicine at New York University's College of Medicine; he formerly had been professor and chairman of the Department of Pathology.* The other researcher was Dr. Aaron Kellner, then associate professor in the Department of Pathology of Cornell University Medical College and director of its central laboratories.

Both of these scientists were well qualified, well respected, and affiliated with excellent medical schools. In the course of their research in pathology, both men had had occasion to inject rabbits with the enzyme papain, and both had observed that the ears of the rabbits collapsed following the injection. Although both of them had observed the floppy ears following the intravenous injection of the rabbits, only one of them went on to discover the explanation for this unusual and amusing event. The reasons for this present a fascinating picture of the conditions under which research usually occurs and what happens to the researchers themselves.

Barber and Fox held interviews with both Dr. Thomas and Dr. Kellner. Let us quote Dr. Thomas, who first noticed the reversible collapse of the rabbits' ears when he was working on the effects of a class of enzymes, the proteolytic enzymes.** Dr. Thomas said,

> I was trying to explore the notion that the cardiac and blood vessel lesions in certain hypersensitivity states may be due to release of proteolytic enzymes. It's an attractive idea on which there's little evidence. And it's been picked up at some time or another by almost everyone working on hypersensitivity. For this investigation I used trypsin, because it was the most available

---

* Dr. Thomas is now president of the Sloan-Kettering Institute for Cancer Research.
** Proteolytic enzymes accelerate the hydrolysis of proteins by catalytic action into simpler organic substances.

enzyme around the laboratory, and I got nothing. We also happened to have papain; I don't know where it had come from; but [because] it was there, I tried it. I also tried a third enzyme, ficin. It comes from figs, and it's commonly used. It has catholic tastes and so it's quite useful in the laboratory. So I had these three enzymes. The other two didn't produce lesions. Nor did papain. But what the papain did was always produce these bizarre cosmetic changes. . . . It was one of the most uniform reactions I'd ever seen in biology. It always happened. And it looked as if something important must have happened to cause this reaction. (19)*

There are several particularly interesting phrases in this initial account of the discovery. For one thing Dr. Thomas said, "For this investigation I used trypsin, because it was the *most available enzyme around the laboratory* . . ." (italics mine). He went on to say, "We also happened to have papain; I don't know where it had come from; but [because] it was there, I tried it." Here, indeed, is accident. They "happened to have" one enzyme and the other was "the most available" around the laboratory. Certainly there was no rigorous, preconceived hypothesis-testing in the choice of these particular enzymes. It was mostly accident that they happened to be in the lab.

Being a good research scientist, Dr. Thomas did not let this unusual event go by. He continued on to describe his immediate search for an explanation:

I chased it like crazy. But I didn't do the right thing . . . I did the expected things. I had sections cut, and I had them stained by all the techniques available at the time. And I studied what I believed to be the constituents of a rabbit's ear. I looked at all the sections, but I couldn't see anything the matter. The connective tissue was intact. There was no change in the amount of elastic tissue. There was no inflammation, no tissue

* Quoted by permission of The University of Chicago Press. Copyright © 1958 by The University of Chicago.

damage. I expected to find a great deal, because I
thought we had destroyed something. (20)

Here another significant phrase appears: "I did the expected
things." He went on and cut the sections and stained them by
all the techniques available at the time of the experiment. He
said that he "expected to find a great deal" because he thought
that something had been destroyed. At the time he also indicated that he had studied the cartilage of the rabbit's ear and
considered it normal. "The cells were healthy-looking and
there were nice nuclei. I decided there was no damage to the
cartilage. And that was that." His examination of the cartilage
had been routine and fairly casual because at that time he did
not entertain the idea seriously that the collapse of the ears
might be associated with cartilage change. "I hadn't thought of
cartilage. You're not likely to, because it's not considered interesting. . . . I know my own idea had always been that cartilage
is a quiet, inactive tissue."

It is undoubtedly true that people do have preconceptions
such as Dr. Thomas had. He thought that there must be some
damage, and found none. He assumed that the damage would
be in the connective or elastic tissues of the ear and shared a
conviction with others that cartilage is "inert and relatively
uninteresting," so he did not pay much attention to it. This
made him unreceptive at the time to the actual explanation for
the floppy ears as changes in the cartilage; he discovered this
explanation accidentally a number of years later.

Dr. Thomas was very anxious to get some explanation for
this uniform biological event, but he finally was obliged to turn
away from his floppy-eared rabbits because he was "terribly
busy working on another problem at the time," a problem with
which he was "making progress." And he also remarked that
he had "already used up all the rabbits I could afford, so I was
able to persuade myself to abandon this other research."

Here are two other impinging events that changed the
course of the research: He was doing other research in which he
was making progress (rewarding to him), and his budget could

not provide for the large number of rabbits he felt he needed in order to pursue this adequately. So he was able to persuade himself to abandon the research with the floppy-eared rabbits and temporarily accept the failure.

Barber and Fox note that it is usual not to report such negative experiments in the scientific literature, for many reasons, not the least of which is the lack of available space for what might be interesting and perhaps valuable experiments but are ones that are not worked out as relatively complete research projects. No one else, therefore, was formally told about Dr. Thomas's work with the floppy-eared rabbits. But he did not forget, and he kept the problem of the floppy ears alive through many informal contacts with colleagues who visited his labs and through other informal meetings. For example, he noted that twice he demonstrated this phenomenon for some of his unbelieving colleagues. As he said, "They didn't believe me when I told them what happened. They didn't really believe that you can get that much change and not a trace of anything having happened when you look in the microscope." The issue remained alive through informal exchanges among scientists.

A couple of years after this accidental discovery, Dr. Thomas was doing another type of experiment. He said,

> I was looking for a way . . . to reduce the level of fibrinogen in the blood of rabbits. I had been studying a form of fibrinoid which occurs inside blood vessels in the generalized Schwartzman reaction and which seems to be derived from fibrinogen. My working hypothesis was that if I depleted the fibrinogen and, as a result, fibrinoid did not occur, this would help. It had been reported that if you inject proteolytic enzymes, this will deplete fibrinogen. So I tried to inhibit the Schwartzman reaction by injecting papain intravenously into the rabbits. It didn't work with respect to fibrinogen. . . . But the same damned thing happened again to the rabbits' ears! (21)

This time, fortunately, Dr. Thomas was able to solve this

puzzle of the floppy ears. He realized that it was an instance of accidental discovery. In his words, this is what happened:

> I was teaching second-year medical students in pathology. We have these small seminars with them: two-hour sessions in the morning, twice a week, with six to eight students. These are seminars devoted to experimental pathology and the theoretical aspects of the mechanism of disease. The students have a chance to see what we, the faculty, are up to in the laboratory. I happened to have a session with the students at the same time that this thing with the rabbits' ears happened again. I thought it would be an entertaining thing to show them . . . a spectacular thing. The students were very interested in it. I explained to them that we couldn't really explain what the hell was going on here. I did this experiment on purpose for them, to see what they would think . . . besides which, I was in irons on my other experiments. There was not much doing on those. I was not being brilliant on these other problems. . . . Well, this time I did what I didn't do before. I simultaneously cut sections of the ears of rabbits after I'd given them papain and sections of normal ears. This is the part of the story I'm most ashamed of. It still makes me writhe to think of it. There was no damage to the tissue in the sense of a lesion. But what had taken place was a quantitative change in the matrix of the cartilage. The only way you could make sense of this change was simultaneously to compare sections taken from the ears of rabbits which had been injected with papain with comparable sections from the ears of rabbits of the same age and size which had not received papain. . . . Before this I had always been so struck by the enormity of the change that when I didn't see something obvious, I concluded there was nothing. . . . Also, I didn't have a lot of rabbits to work with before. (21)

This is one of the major functions that students serve: They remind instructors of the way in which research should have been done originally. Because he was obliged to "do it right," in a sense, and carefully compare normal and papain-injected rabbits' ears as an example for the students, he went on to discover quantitative change in the cartilage, which was the explanation for the floppy ears. Let me quote finally from Dr. Thomas's article (from the *Journal of Experimental Medicine*) in which he reported what had happened to the cartilage in the rabbits' ears. It is quite technical, but this is the final product of years of informal contacts, puzzles, searching, and accident.

> The ear cartilage showed loss of a major portion of the intercellular matrix, and complete absence of basophilia from the small amount of remaining matrix. The cartilage cells appeared somewhat larger and rounder than normal, and lay in close contact with each other. . . . (The contrast between the normal ear cartilage and tissue obtained 4 hours after injection is illustrated in . . . this article.)

What a very formal way to report on the wonderfully human fun and bewilderment which had gone on for so many years in Dr. Thomas's laboratory!

One final interesting accidental discovery was made when Dr. Thomas was demonstrating to students.

> I was so completely sold on the uniformity of this thing that I used the same rabbit (for each seminar). . . . The third time it didn't work. I was appalled by it. The students were there, and the rabbit's ears were still in place. . . . At first I thought that perhaps the technician had given him the wrong stuff. But then when I checked on that and gave the same stuff to the other rabbits and it *did* work I realized that the rabbit had become immune. This is a potentially hot finding. . . . (22)

This was the train of accident and discovery followed by Dr. Thomas. Dr. Kellner, an equally qualified scientist, saw the floppy-eared rabbits when he was working with injections of papain but did not go on to the make the discovery, primarily because the train of discovery led him elsewhere. First of all, Dr. Kellner was interested in muscle tissue and cardiac research. When he observed the changes in the rabbits' ears during some research on heart muscle he said he was "a little curious about it at the time" and "followed it up to the extent of making sections of the rabbits' ears." Here his interest in muscle and preconceived ideas about cartilage (the same as Dr. Thomas's—its inert quality) kept him from seeing further.

> Since I was primarily interested in research questions having to do with the muscles of the heart, I was thinking in terms of muscle. That blinded me, so that changes in the cartilage didn't occur to me as a possibility. I was looking for muscles in the sections, and I never dreamed it was cartilage. (23)

One major influence on Dr. Kellner was the people associated with him in the laboratory, research colleagues who shared his interest in cardiac muscle and reinforced his tendency to move away from the amusing puzzle of the floppy ears to other areas closer to everyone's interest. However, there were also some other serendipitous discoveries about the floppy ears. Among other things, Dr. Kellner was able to discover a blood coagulation defect in papain-injected rabbits, a defect resembling hemophilia in certain respects. So it is possible that serendipity here, while it did not lead to the cartilage explanation of the floppy ears, might have led to other eventual findings of critical importance.

Data Prevail, Not Men

By its very nature science is a mixture of doubt and certainty. I think good scientists should be arrogantly humble. This is not just a play on words; I think they should be arrogant in method and humble in their belief in their knowledge. To psychologists this is particularly applicable. There is so much we do not know as yet in the study of behavior that a proper humility is essential, but this should never lead us to accept unscientific explanations of behavior—such as "human nature"—which conflict with a forthright scientific method. It is better, as Skinner has suggested, to remain without an answer than to accept an inadequate one (124). This is a major characteristic of science—the ability to wait for an answer combined with a continuing search for an explanation and a rejection of premature explanations. Skinner has also suggested other characteristics of science, among these that science is a set of attitudes, "a disposition to deal with the facts rather than with what someone has said about them" (125). Science rejects its own "authorities" when their statements conflict with the observations of natural events. *Data prevail, not men.*

Science, Skinner observes, "is a willingness to accept facts even when they are opposed to wishes" (126). Science places a high premium on honesty,* and incidents of altering data to fit in with a pet theory are unusual. But even accepting the honesty of an investigator, no one firmly committed to a point of view relishes seeing it demolished. If, however, data succeed in destroying treasured beliefs, the scientist accepts the facts even though this involves the loss of an old friend, a bosom theory. The moral here is clear: Do not get involved with proving anything; let the data guide you. As Skinner says, "Experiments do not always come out as one expects, but the facts must stand and the expectations fall. The subject matter, not the scientist, knows best" (127).

I have mentioned that scientists should be arrogant about their methodology while humble about their data. This may create what Martin Gardner has called the "pig-headed orthodoxy" of science, a dedication to methodology that he indi-

---

* In the nineteenth century the famous French mathematician J. L. Lagrange once appeared before a learned society to explain a proof he had worked out for a previously unsolved problem. No sooner had he started to read his paper than he suddenly stopped talking, frowned, and then folded his papers and remarked, "Gentlemen, I must think further about this." This is the self-correcting scientist. We could do very nicely with more paper-folders.

cates is "both necessary and desirable for the health of science (70). This means that the scientist respects facts, and the individual who advances a novel view is required to produce considerable evidence in order to gain recognition of his theories. The world is so full of people who have theories about every conceivable event that scientists could easily spend all their time listening to and refuting the majority of them. There must be some defense against this, for, as Gardner observes, "science would be reduced to shambles by having to examine every new-fangled notion that came along. Clearly, working scientists have more important tasks. If someone announces that the moon is made of green cheese, the professional astronomer cannot be expected to climb down from his telescope and write a detailed refutation."

Admittedly, this pig-headed refusal to examine every theory advanced does make for some martyrs. Men of the caliber of Pasteur have been doubted and attacked. But it is a necessary filter to keep from clogging the wheels of science. And we have faith that ultimately the occasional theory that is correct and is refused an audience will emerge—for, as we have seen, data prevail, not men.

It seems appropriate at this point to comment on what I choose to call *hypothesis myopia,* a common disease among researchers holding certain preconceived ideas that might get in the way of discovery. We have seen this illustrated in the cases of two eminent scientists, Drs. Thomas and Kellner, both of whom failed, at least initially, to make a discovery owing to their preconceived ideas about the inert nature of cartilage. But these researchers missed a point only because they did not immediately go on to find some new facts.

One well-documented case of hypothesis myopia was reported during the time of Galileo. Galileo, in looking through his newly invented telescope, discovered that there were spots on the sun. He presented these findings to his colleagues, and one group, followers of an Aristotelian mode of thought, rejected his data. Their theory of the composition of celestial matter indicated to them that the sun could not possibly have spots, and so they refused to even look through his telescope! Their argument was simple: The sun had no spots; if the telescope showed spots on the sun, then the telescope was distorting the perception. Inasmuch as they knew there were no spots, why should they have bothered to look through an obviously erroneous instrument? Certainly, a first step in such research would have to be a check on the reliability of the telescope. But the Aristotelians were myopic in refusing to make such a check (which could easily have been done in a testable earth situation) and in refusing to allow any questioning of their "certain knowledge" of the sun.

Hypothesis myopia is a disorder of vision, a research nearsightedness in which the sufferer has the facts clearly in view but, because of preconceived notions, either refuses to accept them or attempts to explain them away. Every datum obtained provides information to the prepared mind, which respects data and does not let hypotheses get in the way of research.

CHAPTER
2

Observation and Experimentation

Ultimately, no matter what the scientific discipline, the goal of science is the *understanding* and *control* of its subject matter. The "understanding" part of this pair of concepts may be the easier to accept, because there are sciences that at present have no control of their subject matter—for example, the discipline of astronomy. Astronomy has a highly developed body of knowledge allowing astronomers to describe and predict with high accuracy the movements of stars or the appearance of a comet, but even with these skills of description and prediction astronomy has no way of controlling celestial events; therefore it may be said to be a *descriptive* science.

I have brought into this discussion of the goals of science two aspects related to the goals of understanding and control; these are *description* and *prediction*. Underlying every science are *observation* and *measurement,* which provide the description of events and a way of quantifying them so that experimental manipulation may be achieved. One could say that the two critical foundations of scientific research are observation and *experimentation,* and that measurement provides a meaningful way in which events and their manipulation may be ordered. I will briefly discuss observation and experimentation, offering some comments on prediction, measurement, and the ordering of observation and experimental facts into general laws.

Science is always a balance of observation and experimentation. Observation is the empirical gathering of facts; experimentation is a form of active reasoning about these facts, the manipulation of them for further knowledge, and further observation of them under the controlled experimental condition. Students of science have said that Descartes and Bacon represent opposites in the approach to scientific activity: Descartes did all his work in bed; Bacon experimented in a snow drift, contracted a cold, and, as a result, died at the age of sixty-five. For Descartes, it was possible to have the two elements of fact and reason—crucial to science—without experimentation, yet this is generally not the way science advances. Reason is rooted in observation and extended into experimentation.

Jacob Bronowski has observed that science is a way of describing reality and "is therefore limited by limits of observation, and it asserts nothing which is outside of observation. Anything else is not science. . . ." (34). When he says that science is limited by limits of observation, he is stating one of the boundaries of scientific methodology. The observable is the very keystone of science.

Einstein suggested that the fundamental unit in physics research is *event-signal-observer*. By this he meant that when an event presents some outward manifestation it requires an observer to record it. Certainly, this triad of event-signal-observer is basic to sciences other than physics; scientists, no matter what disciplines they work in, have the responsibility to carefully observe and accurately record the signal that represents the event. For this reason instrumentation has developed. (It has been said the human being is between the atom and the star, and has developed the microscope and telescope to extend the view in both directions.) Instruments serve two main purposes: to provide accurate observation in order to eliminate the bias of the observer, and to extend and quantify the observations of the researcher.

Without proper, accurate instrumentation even the most brilliant scientist cannot obtain all the information potentially to be discovered in the object under study. Let us, for example, take a brief historical look at observation of the planet Saturn. Around 1610, Galileo looked through his crude telescope and observed Saturn. He saw a celestial object with an odd shape, a formation he believed resulted from the presence of two satellites. In his work *Sidereus Nuncius,* Galileo wrote that he had observed the furthest known planet (Saturn) to be a "triplet." Almost half a century later, the Dutch astronomer Christian Huygens improved instrumentation by developing a much superior telescope with a special eyepiece, and in March 1656, he observed the rings of Saturn when they became visible. (Huygens also was able to make accurate predictions as to when the rings would not be visible.) More recently, in 1979, the Pioneer 11 spacecraft, after almost six years in deep space, flew by Saturn, photographed its rings from a half a million miles away, and discovered a new ring, farther out and hidden from earthbound telescopes. Pioneer also tracked what is believed to be a new moon of Saturn. From Galileo, the father of astronomy, to the modern astronomer, able to project his telescope into deep space, is a fantastic change! But the difference is not in talent, brilliance, or approach—it is in the continuing enhancement of techniques of instrumented observation, the engineering of improved perception.

Now, there are certainly problems involved in observation and any discussion of the observed. In 1927 Werner Heisenberg, a German physicist, stated the Uncertainty (or Indeterminacy) Principle, which holds that it is not possible to determine at the same time both the position and speed of an electron. Observers must observe one or the other event. If they choose to observe the position of the electron with complete accuracy, then they must relinquish an accurate evaluation of its speed at that moment, and, conversely, if they wish to study its velocity, they cannot observe its position with accuracy.* The Uncertainty

---

* For a discussion of this point see Margenau (97).

Principle has come to mean that to study an event the observer must interfere with its natural course; as a result, the scientist cannot have all the relevant information at the same time.

Observation

Observation is the first step in gathering information. The statement that observation is basic to science will appear in this book over and over again like a theme in a fugue because it is so important. But what the researcher *does* with his observations is crucial. Science is not a private matter; all scientific information must be public. Fortunately, a major reward for scientists is the recognition by their peers that they have contributed to the body of knowledge in their field; hence publication of research information in journals and other avenues of communication.

Also basic to our view of observation is the all-important aspect of *description,* for description as an objective reporting of events is essential to scientific communication. "Objective reporting" is the key phrase. Subjective evaluations that color reporting are unscientific. I recall a ward nurse entering on the chart of a patient, "Mrs. X sat in the hall for ages." Here we may invoke the admonition of the *New Yorker* magazine: "Just give us the news; never mind the editorial." How long is "ages"? Does not this report tell us much more about the observer than the observed by the very nature of the comment? To be sure, such reporting is common and can be colorful, but it is not appropriate in scientific reporting.

A critical requirement of observation is that it be *replicable;* that is, the same event must be seen, recorded, and reported by others. This is what is meant by a *data language* in science. A simple example would be meter-pointer readings, where one observer can report an alteration in a meter needle and have this observation repeated by others. The more accurate the instrument of measurement, the closer the replication of observation can be.

One of the basic problems in the field of psychology has

been the lack of a universal data language to which observations may be related and in which they may be expressed. Obviously, one talks differently about a disordered personality than one talks about a deflection of three degrees in a needle. The margin of error in the former description is great; in the latter it is minimal. Psychology's need for a data language to sharpen observation has been considered by Joel Greenspoon (73) and R. C. Davis (53), who both suggest physical referents for psychological observation and description. The data language of psychology will be discussed in a bit more detail in the section on operational methods (Chapters 6-7).

I suggest that if the observation is not clear or replicable within the defined limits of observation, it is not liable to scientific study. It may become so in the future when instrumentation enlarges the ability to measure and observe, but this in no way changes the immediate criterion for scientific boundaries. As we saw in discussing the characteristics of science, one should wait for an answer rather than create an inadequate one.

Observation, then, is ideally expressed in an objective and clear description of the events observed. The observation leads to a description which itself becomes data. For example, in anthropology the careful reporting of a tribal ritual offers documentation of an event that other anthropologists can read and evaluate in the light of similar reports. In this way an anthropological researcher can formulate a conceptual scheme in which similarities as well as differences among different events may be analyzed and general principles formulated.

We have seen that descriptions based on observation can lead to the formulation of testable hypotheses, the very basis of the scientific method. Thus, the hypotheses derived from objective observation and description form the basis for experimentation.

Let us discuss some of the forms of scientific observation.

Types of Observation

Naturalistic observation. A frequently used means of gathering information is that of *naturalistic observation,* in which investigators bring their observational skills to bear in studying behavior in a natural setting. Marine biologists interested in studying migration patterns in lobsters would not perform a laboratory experiment, but would take their instruments of observation to the scene in which such behaviors occur (which means that in addition to biological research skills they would have to have the ability to dive with underwater gear). They would take precautions that their presence would not act as a major interference—that is, disturb the normal patterns of migration in the subjects they were studying. Some disturbance, however, would be inevitable; to study migration the marine biologist would wish to identify individuals, hence the lobsters would have to be tagged with identifying markers. A classic example of naturalistic observation is that of Jane Goodall's study of African chimpanzees (141). After almost two years of living in the natural forest environment—the chimpanzees' habitat—she was finally able to come close enough to the chimpanzees to observe them without significantly disturbing their normal patterns. Similarly, Devore and Washburn's studies of baboons in the animals' native veldts yielded extremely important information about baboon behavior (56).

It is interesting to compare the findings of the naturalists studying baboons in their natural habitat with earlier studies by Zuckerman of baboons in the London Zoo (153). The caged zoo animals obviously were subjected to different stimulus conditions from those of the baboons in their natural habitat. The caged animals exhibited high-frequency sexual behaviors and aggression, which were not seen with the same frequencies in the natural living environment, where more varied behaviors were possible.

However, the combination of controlled and naturalistic observation can be an important source of information about behavior. Although we have used animal examples of naturalistic observation, a similar type of observation can be made in human settings such as nursery schools, where children can be observed under like circumstances. Again, investigators must assure that their presence does not alter the subjects' normal behavioral patterns.

Case Studies. Another investigative technique is the *case study,* in which information is collected about the behavior of an individual or group observed over a period of time. A case study may be viewed as a special type of naturalistic observation. Reporting an instance of disease or disorder in one individual— which yields important information for a clinical practitioner —is a type of study reported in clinical journals. Clinical psychologists often use the case study method for analyzing the behaviors of an individual patient or group of patients on a ward; they use various types of information gathering, such as observation, interviewing, psychological testing, and correlation of information from other professionals such as social workers and psychiatrists.

At times, the case study can be a very detailed and long-range one; for example, the sociological analysis of physicians and patients of a particular metabolic ward reported by Fox (66). The patients were suffering from diseases neither well understood nor treatable by then-current medical techniques. The study of the interactions of patients and physicians, how each coped with stress, and the effect on ward personnel and other patients of a patient dying yielded important sociological information about ward behaviors. The investigator carefully observed and reported events, but could not alter them through manipulation. It would seem that in this way a case study is indeed another form of a naturalistic observation, with added techniques of interviewing and similar information-gathering methods. In psychology it is an important technique.

I believe it important at this point to emphasize that to make a scientific contribution observations in the natural setting or in more controlled settings such as a hospital ward must be collated with similar reports so that a body of data emerges. As I have mentioned, the anthropologist who reports a single event contributes one piece to an overall picture of ritual. Case reports should begin to build a body of information about a disease process. In this manner we achieve the scientific goal of ordering facts so that general principles and laws of behavior develop.

Observation also may (and usually does) lead to experimentation, in which the elements of an observed-described event may be subjected to manipulation so that an explanation of the event may be obtained. Let us now examine *experimentation* in the scientific method.

Experimentation

The experimental approach is basically a laboratory technique that involves rigid control of *variables*. A variable is an event that may vary from time to time and from condition to condition; experimenters begin by setting up and formally controlling any variables that might affect their results. An experiment is a progression of *independent variables* manipulated by the experimenter, each studied as a probable cause of the ultimate result of the experimental manipulation, the *dependent variable*. An example would be a change in behavior resulting from the application of a particular technique—such as improved performance on a test as a result of certain changes in study behavior. The independent variables are subject to experimental manipulation. For example, an investigator might wish to compare programmed learning—in which students pace themselves and work alone with a program—to learning from standard lectures given by an instructor. To make this comparison, the investigator would have to make many careful experimental manipulations. Certainty would have to be established that the amount of information in the lecture be the same as the amount in the individualized instruction for comparisons to be meaningful; the printed material in the program should not contain more or less bits of information than were in the lecture. The independent variable in this instance is the type of presentation of the information (program or lecture); the dependent variable is the student's performance on an examination, that is, how much of the information conveyed was retained and produced by the student for each type of presentation.

Thus, the fundamental model for experimental research is the development of an *experimental group* (in our learning example above, the group receiving programmed instruction) compared with a *control group* (the group receiving the standard lecture). Obviously for such a comparison to be fruitful the groups would have to be matched on another set of variables, such as age, grade level, grade-point average, and similar elements.

In a detailed experiment on the effects of papain on the rabbits' ears (18), for example, Thomas would have been required to set up an experimental group of papain-injected animals and a control group of animals injected with an inert substance such as saline water. (That's one way of splitting hares!)

Now let us take a more detailed example. Suppose you wish to study the possible effects of smoking marijuana on the ability to drive an automobile. You would proceed first by making certain that you were working with a quantified strength of marijuana. The active ingredient in marijuana is tetrahydrocannabinol (THC), and the amount varies with the source. For example, marijuana from Iowa has less measurable THC than marijuana from Hawaii, and therefore is less psychoactive—that is, capable of producing intoxication. Whatever the strength, the experimenter must be assured that a definite, known, standard level of THC is present in the marijuana used in the study. In most experiments, pure THC is used to insure quantifiable data.

Here you run into an element of uncertainty that is known as an *uncontrolled variable*—that is, an individual's susceptibility to such stimulants. People vary in their susceptibility to drugs, so you would need to select subjects for comparison who are as much alike as possible on important variables such as sex, age, driving skill, and drug susceptibility. At best this is a difficult task; therefore, most experimenters rely on *sampling,* a procedure in which a part of a population with which one is concerned is studied and inferences are then made regarding the total population. The experimenter would have to control for many variables, such as drug strength, the drug susceptibility of an individual, and an individual's experience in use of the drug. Perhaps one of the questions to be answered would be,

"Does a subject experienced with marijuana show a different effect from a subject who has never smoked?" Finally, precautions would have to be taken that ensure that subjects do not know whether they are smoking marijuana or, perhaps, simple tobacco. To control for this, the experimenter would use a vehicle such as flavoring to disguise the taste.

The experimental group proposed here would receive marijuana; the other group is used as a control and would not receive the drug. The control group might receive nothing or, as suggested above, a tobacco made indistinguishable from true marijuana by its taste and smell. The reason for the latter is a simple one: Subjects may develop expectations that will affect their performance. Knowing that they received the THC and another group did not (never underestimate the speed with which an experiment is publicized), the subjects in the experimental group might believe that certain events were supposed to happen following the ingestion of the agent. Therefore, a control group taking a substance is needed, and neither group should know what it is receiving. The flavored tobacco as a control for the THC is known as a *placebo* because, ideally, it appears identical to the experimental agent administered. Through its use any expectations other than those about the effects of marijuana would be ruled out. ("Placebo" means "I please" in Latin and comes from the medical practice, particularly in years past, of giving patients a "sugar pill" to make them feel that they had received a treatment when in the physician's judgment they needed none.)

These procedures probably seem involved and naive in many ways, but to study the effects of marijuana on driving skills they would be necessary. The independent variable is marijuana, the dependent variable is driving performance. Here, quantification is also crucial; having subjects go out and drive cars is not only poorly standardized as a measurable dependent variable, but could also be quite hazardous. Therefore the experimenter uses a simulator—an enclosed booth equipped with the elements of driving, such as a steering wheel, brakes, and a screen on which is projected the "road" the subject is negotiating. Such a film can produce events such as the sudden appearance of a child running onto the road; the element of braking can be measured precisely as a response to that stimulus. In this way the dependent variable is broken down from the abstract "driving performance" to specific and measurable behaviors.

The hypothesis that marijuana will have an effect on driving skills can then be answered after these experimental manipulations. This is a basic design, a "grass-roots" experiment if you will, illustrating experimental and control groups and the complexity of identifying and controlling variables.

One of the characteristics of studies of this type is that the behavior can be quantified. In this study driving skill is a measurable behavior. But suppose you had a "matched" group study in which a new drug was being tested on a ward. One group of patients would receive the therapeutic agent to be tested, and a matched control group would receive a placebo. Here you would run into a confounding variable. The drug and the placebo would probably be administered to the subject patient by a ward nurse. If the administering personnel and the personnel involved in the study know which patients received the true drug and which received the placebo, their observations might be colored by expectations. That is, their reporting of patient behavior might be a result of observations confounded by subjective expectations of success or failure with the drug. These observer biases are often controlled by what is known clinically as a *double-blind* experiment, in which the nurses administering the drug or placebo do not know what they are giving the patients and the patients do not know what they are receiving. Sometimes this type of experiment has been unkindly referred to as a "triple-blind" experiment, because the experimenter too does not know what he is doing!

Correlational Studies: Controlled Observation

There are many situations in which it is not possible to manipulate independent variables. We have used marijuana as an example of an independent variable used to study its effects on skilled behaviors. However, some individuals might consider this exposure of human subjects to marijuana to be questionable ethics. But there are even clearer instances in which one could not ethically deliberately expose human subjects to certain independent variables. For example, in recent years concern has been growing about the effect of pollutants and other toxic agents on the biology and behavior of exposed humans. Asbestos, for example, is an important agent for retarding fire, and as such is a safety device. Yet evidence has grown that individuals exposed to certain levels of asbestos can develop pulmonary problems. Obviously, there is no ethical way that human subjects can be divided into experimental and control groups, with one group exposed and the other not exposed to asbestos, for the purpose of measuring some dependent variable such as pulmonary changes. Accordingly, the investigator turns to a *correlational study* to determine whether the two events co-exist and co-vary.

Correlation is a means of establishing the relationship existing among two or more observed events, variables, or scores. A correlation indicates that individual attributes in separate measurements tend to vary together. Thus, a perfect correlation is obtained when the scores on one variable can be proved to vary consistently with the scores on another variable. An example of such a relationship is that of educational level and income; studies have demonstrated that a high level of education is correlated with a high level of income.

With this in mind, let us return to the ethics of exposing human subjects to asbestos for experimental purposes. A recent report by Joseph Bellanca examined such asbestos-related diseases as asbestosis to consider correlations among variables (24). (Asbestosis is a disease in which exposure to asbestos causes a gradual increase in fibrous connective lung tissue, a consequence that leads to loss of elasticity in the lung, difficulty in breathing, and, eventually, heart disease.) Heavy exposures to asbestos have been positively correlated with asbestosis. In the course of these studies, another correlational effect appeared: Workers who were exposed to heavy asbestos levels *and* who were heavy cigarette smokers developed lung cancer, but workers who were nonsmokers did not show an increased risk of cancer even though they had contracted asbestosis. Thus a three-way correlation appeared: smoking/asbestosis/cancer of the lung. This is typical of correlative studies that trace variables and their relationship; they coexist, but no statement is made about cause and effect. To state a cause-effect relationship, one must manipulate variables experimentally in the manner previously described.

And so we return to the ethical question: How can you perform an experiment in which you expose subjects to high levels of asbestos and manipulate variables to determine possible causation of fibrosis and lung cancer? You could perhaps ethically experiment on animals, but this brings to bear the question of generalizability; that is, could you say with a good level of confidence that a mouse exposed to asbestos (or hair sprays or saccharin) that develops cancer would be a basis for warning humans? Indeed, this has been done. For example, the label on a sugar-free soft drink says, "Use of this product may be hazardous to your health. This product contains saccharin, which has been determined to cause cancer in laboratory animals."

Sometimes, however, a correlation can be the basis of a human experiment, as, for example, in the relationship of aspirin and coronary disease.

Laboratory research and clinical observation of correlations can form a basis for experimentation. Laboratory studies a decade ago demonstrated that aspirin reduces platelet aggregation, that is, the clotting action of blood (101). Animal studies showed identical findings (146). And clinical observations suggested that arthritic human patients had a lower incidence of coronary heart disease than might be expected in the normal population. One of the major factors differentiating arthritic from normal individuals was the high amount of aspirin they ingested to ease arthritic pain. Coupling this observation with aspirin's known anticlotting mechanism made the hypothesis that aspirin can prevent coronaries a logical derivation.

The experimental design resulting from these observations would require an experimental group that received a specified amount of aspirin and a control group that received a placebo. The matching of these groups for age and medical history would also be essential, and to assure that the experiment was a successful clinical trial one would need large numbers of subjects. Such design requirements were met by the Coronary Drug Project Aspirin Study, which coordinated experiments both in central laboratories and in fifty-three clinical centers (49). This project was followed by others in which promising results with aspirin were found.

A recent Canadian study of aspirin as a possible preventive agent in stroke revealed an interesting finding (42). In this study a total of 585 patients, male and female, were studied in twenty-four clinical centers. The finding was that aspirin reduced the risk of continuing ischemic (blood-clotting) attacks in males by 48 percent, but there was no statistically significant reduction in female subjects. Thus, another research question emerges: Why not in females? A possible answer is to be found in recent work on prostaglandin synthesis and its interaction with aspirin, a most complex event and one with implications for differences between men and women.

Whether or not aspirin turns out to be a successful preventive agent in heart attacks—because of its easy availability, simple ingestion, and low cost it would make a desirable therapy—the above oversimplified account of aspirin research illustrates the scientific method. The complexity of the studies can be appreciated: The orchestration of human laboratory experiments and clinical trials in experiments with laboratory animals represents the ideal in coordinating scientific information about a clinical problem. Aspirin, which is normally a well-tolerated drug, does not present an ethical issue. About the only ethical issue that might be raised is a question regarding the placebo group: One might ask the question, if there is reason to believe that aspirin prevents heart attacks, should not *all* of the subjects have been given the drug? But if this position had been taken, the answer to the experimental question could not have been obtained and our information regarding the efficacy of the therapy would not be available.

In this chapter we have seen that careful observation can provide the basis for evaluating events and their relationships with other events. More important is the role that precisely described observation plays in developing the basis for experimentation.

CHAPTER
3

Experience and Experiment

So far we have talked about the science of psychology as dependent upon the experimental method, in which careful observation leads to the experimental manipulation of variables to confirm or refute hypotheses. But many psychologists who know and respect the experimental method nonetheless believe it may not be entirely appropriate or relevant to their field.

The Humanistic Psychologist

An example of this group may be found in the school of humanistic psychologists, who believe that psychology should be a service-oriented discipline aimed toward an approach that, as James Bugental says, "cares about man." Continuing, he says that humanistic psychology "values meaning more than procedure." It is concerned less with methodology than with the "meaningfulness to the human condition of the issues with which it deals." The humanistic position, Bugental says, "looks for human rather than nonhuman validation." The humanist does not reject the use of statistical methods or tests by experimentation, but does "insist that these are but means, and that the ultimate criterion must be that of human experience" (40).

Experience plays a large role in the orientation of the humanist, which derives largely from the existentialist philosophies of
Kierkegaard, Camus, and Sarte, and more recent theorists such
as Maslow. Experience is all-important to these theorists in that
it represents the human being, distinguished from other animals
by phenomenology, ability to exist with a consciousness of self,
and unique personal experience that others cannot fully comprehend. The ultimate criterion for humanists such as Bugental
"must be that of human experience and, again, the ultimate
focus of our concern is the experience of the human being."

This is a manifestly reasonable and legitimate position. The
humanistic psychologist, focusing on human experience as the
main source of concern, rejects controlled experimentation that
isolates, for example, stimuli and responses. The human focus
would suggest that animal experimentation is at best irrelevant
and at worst interfering, because it directs energy away from
the study of human experience. As Bugental notes, humanistic
psychology "looks for human rather than nonhuman validation" and, in another observation, he says that "humanistic
psychology disavows the sort of scientific detachment pre-
tended to or achieved at great cost by other orientations."
Thus, the sought-after objectivity of the experimentalist is less
desirable than the acceptance of the human being's subjective
awareness of his own condition. Such an orientation clearly
dictates research methodology in which no animal experiments
are relevant; statistical methods, although not disavowed, are
not as meaningful as the introspective examination of the
human experience—hence the phenomenological emphasis.

Scientific method—especially as espoused by behaviorists—
is seen to be "dehumanizing" because it reduces behavior to a
set of principles common to animal and human—for example,
in experiments on learning where similarities among different
species are seen as evidence for the lawful nature of behavior.
The humanistic psychologist is more likely to use a case study or
a verbal report than to conduct a variable-controlled experiment.
As Cronbach has said, the nonexperimentalist "is in love with
just those variables the experimenters left home to forget" (50).

My discussion here may suggest that the techniques and conceptual schemes of the humanist and the experimentalist are poles apart and irreconcilable. This is not necessarily so, although, just as the humanist may believe the experimental scientist dehumanizes psychologial events, the converse may occur —the experimentalist may believe that the humanistic psychologist "descience-izes" the world of psychology. It is true that the methods differ, but even here some accommodation is possible and indeed may strengthen the approaches of both. Sidney Jourard, for example, has suggested that in human research a mutual "self-disclosure" by experimenter and subjects may be a valuable technique (83). In such an approach the subjects would be asked to report their perceptions of the stimuli presented by the experimenter, their responses, and what each means to them. The experimenters would also verbalize their perceptions of the subjects' behavior as the subjects respond to the experimental situation. Jourard thus believes the experimental method of controlled observation and experimentation would be enhanced rather than damaged by experiential information provided by both experimenter and subjects. This is not always possible—nor indeed always desirable—but the approach has merit as a means of providing further data to an experiment. In addition, it has the obvious advantages of telling the experimenters how their experiments are perceived, providing a more open approach, and, as Jourard observes, changing the position of the subject from that of "an anonymous *object* of our study to that of a *person,* a fellow seeker, a *collaborator* in our enterprise" (83).

The latter point is crucial. Duane Schultz discovered that around 80 percent of the subjects in psychological experiments are drawn from the college population, a rather distorted source in terms of the general population (112). But the important point here is that students who act as subjects should have the opportunity to learn psychological reasoning and methods while acting as subjects. Placing them more in the role of collaborator has the added advantage of rendering the scientific experiment a teaching experience as well.

Partnership among psychologists of all persuasions is crucial for a better understanding of human behavior. Just as we
expect experimentalists to be aware of their subjects as individuals while preserving a scientific approach, we can ask the
humanist to understand the relevance of experimentation. Perhaps the best approach is that suggested by the poet Shelley,
who in his *Defence of Poetry* has noted that one of the tasks of
the artist or poet is to "absorb the new knowledge of sciences
and assimilate it to human needs, color it with human passions,
transform it into the blood and bone of human nature."

The Private Made Public

It is true that much of what appears private and unapproach-
able from an experimental standpoint—the personal experience
of an individual—might well lend itself to experimental analysis. Such a private experiential event that has been the subject
of experimental research is dreaming.

In the *Upanishads* of ancient India, existence takes three
forms—one in this world, one in the spiritual world, and one in
the world of dreams. How in the world would experimental scientists apply research methods to so private an experience as a
dream? They might, as Calvin Hall did, try an observational,
correlational approach (76). Hall collected ten thousand
dreams from "normal"—that is, non-psychiatric—subjects.
His interpretations of their dreams did not take a psychoanalytic turn, using symbolism (for instance: water tower =
phallic symbol); rather, he viewed each dream as a verbal
report by—and creation of—the dreamer, reflecting the
dreamer's perceptions of him- or herself and the world. The
dreamer is responsible for everything that appears in the dream
—he or she thought of it. And Hall states emphatically that
dreams must be read in series rather than in isolation, to see
how they all tie together as a coherent theme.

To begin the analysis, one makes a tally of events, which
covers mainly dream settings, dream action, actors, and plots.
Settings, Hall found, were mostly prosaic—houses, streets, and

stores—but were rarely work sites, such as offices or factories. Actors were tallied in a number of ways—older males (that is, older than the dreamer), older females, peer males and females, and younger males and females. Animals and inanimate objects were also tallied. The dream actions were mostly those associated with the dreamer's waking life. An interesting and perhaps disturbing finding from the study was that aggressive and negative emotions were expressed in dreams far more frequently than positive, happy emotions.

What we have so far is a means of approaching dreams as action-reporting without preliminary interpretation. In a series of ten dreams a dreamer may have a predominant setting of a home and deal aggressively with older males and positively with peer females. This can be a theme on which to base further interpretation, a highly private event rendered observable through reporting.

Another approach to the private experience of dreaming and sleeping has been the use of electrophysiology. Before 1953, when Eugene Aserinsky and Nathaniel Kleitman of the University of Chicago published a paper on sleep research (3), it was generally believed that there are two states of consciousness in the animal world, wakefulness and sleep. Aserinsky and Kleitman applied to this research techniques of electrophysiology, with which they measured electrical impulses through the electroencephalograph (which amplifies electroactivity in the brain and produces an ink tracing). They also placed electrodes on the eyelids of sleeping subjects, and were thus able to measure eye motility, that is, movement of the eye during sleep. These investigators pioneered a field of research which has burgeoned in the last three decades—the study of "rapid-eye-movement" (REM) sleep as contrasted with "non-rapid-eye-movement" (NREM) sleep. They found within a period of seven to eight hours that there are four or more periods of emergence from deeper sleep stages: Stage 1 is the lightest stage, close to wakefulness; Stage 4 is close to coma. During a period of normal sleep, subjects were found to emerge from deeper stages back to Stage 1; as morning neared, lighter sleep periods became progressively longer while deeper sleep became progressively shorter. Sleep patterns varied among individuals and for the same person on different nights. Stages 2, 3, and 4—the deeper sleep stages—were normally accompanied by slow eye movements or ocular quiescence; the emergent stage 1—the lightest stage—was associated with rapid, jerky eye movements, often in clusters. Each of these REM stages lasted about twenty minutes, and averaged four each night.

Other physiological events were measured during sleep in a number of studies. During the REM periods the level of activity in other parts of the body also was found to be raised; respiration, blood pressure, and oxygen consumption were higher, and autonomic nervous system activity was also increased.

A recent study by J. Allen Hobson, Theodore Spagna, and Robert Malenka used both electroencephalographic recordings and time-lapse photography to study postural immobility and sleep cycle phases in human subjects (79). One of their findings was that the longest periods of postural immobility are associated with the NREM phase of the sleep cycle. This finding further documents the physiological activity associated with REM sleep.

We have briefly considered several approaches to make observable the highly private experience of sleeping and dreaming, from Hall's correlational tallies of dreaming events to the instrumentation of electrophysiology represented by the early work of Aserinsky and Kleitman and the more recent work of Hobson and his colleagues. The use of experimental techniques to make such a private event public appears most relevant and meaningful.

The criteria for scientific research were clearly met in the discussed dream studies. Observations, at times enhanced by quantified instrumentation (such as that of electrophysiology), were made under controlled conditions, or in correlational studies that had clearly defined criteria in mind (Hall). In either situation the replicability of the research was clear.

Problems in Parapsychology

In another important area of human experience that we will now discuss, there is no such clarity regarding replicability, experimental control, or observation, yet large numbers of people fully believe in it—that is, the experiential field of parapsychology, extrasensory perception (ESP), and telepathy. No doubt there are investigators in parapsychology who are diligent, industrious, and creative. At the moment, however, despite the use of scientific tools such as experimental design and statistical proof, there are factors that place parapsychology beyond the boundaries of science. One of these is the problem of observer replicability. For example, the failure of one investigator to achieve results with a particular experimental subject while another apparently gets good results in terms of high scoring on extrasensory perception tasks has been explained as a problem in attitude. An experimenter who is hostile to the hypothesis of extrasensory perception will supposedly not get good results, while a sympathetic experimenter will. The assumption —as yet unproved—is that these attitudes in some way affect the mental activity of the subject.

Though it may sound unnecessarily restrictive, one must say that the data of parapsychology cannot be admitted as scientific data until the observations become consistent from experimenter to experimenter under specified conditions and with control of the variables. This is not to condemn such data to a limbo from which they cannot return. It simply means that Bronowski's observation about the nonscientific character of events outside of observation must be kept in view in evaluating such research, even though the experiments may be carefully conceived and executed.

Proponents of parapsychology have insisted that because the power of extrasensory perception is so delicate and fleeting it can only appear in research in which there are positive attitudes and friendly feelings toward the area. In addition, the fleeting nature of the ability to perform such tasks makes it sporadic and difficult to repeat from one research setting to another. Critics of ESP, such as Persi Diaconis (57), have commented negatively on ESP research because of its sporadic appearance and its need for a friendly environment, as well as what Diaconis calls its "common association with fraud."

Diaconis is a professional magician as well as a professor of statistics and has used his skills of magic to observe what he considers to be fraud during some demonstrations of ESP.

Another magician, who is also a distinguished mathematician, is Martin Gardner, who analyzed a special power reported in the literature and found it wanting (68). Individuals were given materials such as newspapers that they were able to "see" with their fingers. A twenty-two-year-old Russian woman read print by moving a fingertip over the lines, and in the United States a young woman while blindfolded identified the colors of test cards and bits of cloth simply by rubbing them with her fingers. These accounts were indeed sensational. In another episode a "mentalist" appeared on television and at civic club meetings in Phoenix, Arizona, demonstrating his ability to read, while blindfolded, such items as the serial numbers on dollar bills. All of these professed abilities seem interesting and certainly deserve to be studied and explained. But the first step in such a case is to examine the control over the normal senses. In this regard, control of the experimental methodology appears to have been nonexistent.

Gardner, in his incisive article on perception with the fingertips (referred to as dermo-optical perception, or DOP), indicates quite clearly that it is virtually impossible to put a blindfold on an individual (particularly a person experienced in this area) to prevent a line of vision down the sides of the nose (68). In his article, subtitled "A Peek Down the Nose," Gardner reports on the technique used by blindfolded magicians who, while pretending to concentrate, raise their heads slightly and peek down the nose through two tiny apertures that allow them to see. They often hold the bridge of the nose between their fingers while "concentrating," for further manipulation of the blindfold. The very structure of the human face, of the cheekbones in particular, makes it virtually impossible to obtain a perfect seal using a blindfold. As Gardner indicates, any experienced person can achieve enough of an aperture to be able to see—despite putty, gauze, bandages, or any other technique used to blindfold. For an apparatus that effectively blindfolds,

Gardner suggests an aluminum box with airholes at the top and a shoulder harness, resting so that the individual cannot peek down his nose. Regarding "reading" by fingertip, when such adequate precautions were taken (which meant more than the simple type of blindfold mask used), the results were negative.

Such methodology leaves us with no information as to whether it is indeed possible for individuals to read with their fingertips or through extrasensory powers. Correctly designed experiments are crucial to answering important problems and questions such as these. Although parapsychologists are perfectly correct in asking for acceptance of demonstrated experimentation, the body of science is also correct in demanding that this experimentation be accurate, appropriate, and rigorous.

A major difficulty posed by parapsychology is its acceptance of a dualistic position in which mind and body are viewed as separate, though interrelated, entities. This view removes parapsychology completely from the natural sciences. I have no intention of getting involved in a rehash of the mind-body problem at this point—this book is too short for that—but I will state that psychology, as a science, must accept the monistic position of science and reject the temptation to deal with mental events as though they existed separately from physical ones. This position has proved successful in other sciences, and fits into the search for order and uniformity basic to scientific methodology. To establish a second realm of the mental confounds the science. The argument that there are intrinsically (and fundamentally) psychic events—such as thought processes and dreams—again confounds the issue, because the study of these events must proceed along lines established in science.

Parapsychology is not alone in suffering from the problem of observer replication. Many areas of psychology labor under this handicap, largely, as I have said, because there is no clear data language that would allow for (or create) observer agreement. Parapsychology gets different results from a subject under different experimental conditions and with different experimenters. This variability of performance, although regrettable, is not unusual. What seems to exclude parapsychology from the body of science is its initial assumption of *para*normal events, illustrated in the term *extra*sensory perception. The initial assumption is that the data of parapsychology start outside normal events, and investigation has always been directed by this assumption. But science starts with the basic statement that events in nature, including behavior, are ordered and lawful and that the goal of a scientist is the search for order and similarity.

I believe—this is obviously my own predilection—that the study of telepathy could legitimately start with a more intensive study of normal perception, not with an initial statement of the paranormal. Even the most dedicated spiritualist dealing with departed souls uses physical avenues of sight and hearing to conjure up spirits. Do people report visions? Very well, start with a thorough examination of the normal perception of such individuals. If the horizons are then extended to study visions seen outside space and time, so be it, as long as you have begun with a search for order and have not ignored the most economical of explanations. The person who offers an explanation dramatically outside the current body of law in a science has the burden of proof. No one can expect a scientist to accept evidence for the reincarnation of souls without scientifically obtained proof, and this does not mean anecdotes about ghosts or previous existences. The difficulties encountered in approaching such problems scientifically are illustrated by Ian Stevenson's essay on the fate of the "deceased personality" and reincarnation (136).

To follow the hypotheses it is imperative that the experimental methodologies and apparatus be proper and appropriate. This position of rejecting observations lying outside scientific boundaries may seem narrow and harsh, but, again, the burden of proof is on the person presenting such observations. This often creates a martyr to scientific rigidity (such as Pasteur or Koch or Semmelweiss), but ultimately, as we have seen, data prevail, not men. Sometimes the martyr seems to present a reasoned and reasonable case, as in the following quotation:

> To me truth is precious. . . . I should rather be right
> and stand alone than to run with the multitude and be
> wrong. . . . The holding of views herein set forth has
> already won for me the scorn and contempt and ridi-
> cule of some of my fellow men. I am looked upon as
> being odd, strange, peculiar. . . . But truth is truth and
> though all the world reject it and turn against me, I
> will cling to truth still.

These impressive and brave sentences are taken from a book by
Charles de Ford published in 1931 in which he proves the earth
is flat (55). Gardner's statement (quoted on pp. 17–18) about
the necessary pig-headed orthodoxy of science cannot be better
illustrated than by this quotation from de Ford. If one's information differs from the ordered information of the relevant
science, then one's responsibility is to offer proof. Then the
responsibility of science is to listen.

CHAPTER

4

Reason From Experiment: Toward Order and Law

The first step in the scientific method, then, is observation or empirical gathering of facts. But facts themselves are not enough; they are merely the first step. As I have mentioned, comprehending order through reasoned activity is essential to the achievement of the ultimate goals of science. Science is by no means merely a collection of isolated facts, no matter how accurately they have been observed and recorded. It is the search for consistency and order among the facts that characterizes the scientific method.* To record X, Y, and Z accurately is indeed the critical first step, but science eventually has to describe the similarities existing among variables and their functional relationships. As Bronowski has observed, "the truth of science is not truth to fact, which can never be more than approximate, but the truth of the laws which we see within the facts" (32).

---

* In 1848, Renan wrote in *L'Avenir de la Science* [The Future of Science]: "All the special sciences start by the affirmation of unity, and only begin to distinguish when analysis has revealed numerous differences where before had been visible nothing but uniformity. Read the Scottish psychologists, and you will find at each page that the primary rule of the philosophical method is to maintain distinct that which is distinct, not to anticipate facts by a hurried reduction to unity, not to recoil before the multiplicity of causes" (111).

Scientists move from the careful observation of events to a search for order, for consistencies and uniformities, for functional, lawful relationships among the events. They attempt to find more and more information that will relate events within some meaningful and consistent order. They require uniformity of events. Bronowski has said,

> We cannot define truth in science until we move from fact to law. And within the body of laws in turn, what impresses us as truth is the orderly coherence of the pieces. They fit together like the characters in a great novel, or like the words in a poem. Indeed, we should keep that last analogy by us always. For science is language and, like a language, it defines its parts by the way they make up a meaning. Every word in the sentence has some uncertainty of definition, and yet the sentence defines its own meaning and that of its words conclusively. It is the eternal unity and coherence of science which give it truth, and which make it a better system of prediction than any less orderly language. (33)

As Bronowski suggests, in this sense science becomes a language for describing nature. It begins with a statement of faith and a commitment to order. This is no less true of psychology and the study of behavior than of physics or chemistry. Psychologists cannot function effectively as scientists unless they accept the assumption that behavior is lawful and understandable. Psychology, as a scientific discipline, accepts the general tenet of the lawfulness and uniformity of natural events, a tenet that every other science has discovered to be a critical foundation.

Observation has taken us to experimentation and experimentation has taken us to the search for order and uniformity upon which we may base laws. Murray Sidman offers an interesting account of a personal experience that illustrates the importance of uniformities in scientific methodology.

As a young graduate student . . . I felt that my work
had to be different, that it had to produce something
new that would startle the world. Along these lines I
once wrote a paper, describing some of my work in
which I emphasized how different my experiments were
from anything else that had ever been done. One of my
teachers, W. N. Schoenfeld, agreed that the data were
very interesting. But he went on to add that I had written the paper from a peculiar point of view. I had
emphasized the *differences* between my work and
everyone else's. But science does not ordinarily advance that way. It is the job of science to find orderly
relations among phenomena, not differences. It would
have been more useful if I could have pointed out the
similarities between my work and previous experiments. (115)*

This does not mean, by any stretch of the imagination, that
scientists are attempting to conform. Nor are they trying merely
to repeat the experiments of others or question experimental
data that others may have achieved. Far from it. It means
simply that the more we can develop concepts of likeness and
orderly relationship among events, the closer we are to effective
prediction and control of our science. When we discover, for
example, the likenesses that exist between the bacillus, the
virus, and the crystal, or the functional similarities that may
exist among the cell and the organism and society, we move
closer to effective prediction.

Prediction From Observation and Experiment

I have noted that science is a technique for ordering events into
lawful relationships, and that the goals of science are understanding, prediction, and control based on such lawfulness. A
law, as it is usually described, is a collection of facts grouped
into a consistent body of knowledge from which it is possible

---

* Quoted by permission of Basic Books, Inc.

to make predictions. But it is obvious that no prediction is completely certain, because it is not possible to know all the variables operating in a particular situation. All we ask of a prediction is that it be based on a lawful ordering of events and that it forecast, as accurately as possible, what will happen in a future event within as narrow a range of uncertainty as possible.

This introduces the basic concept of *probability,* which is fundamental to scientific method. When we talk about the probabilities of an event occurring, we are, in a sense, giving odds, saying the chances are that if X is manipulated in a certain fashion, Y will change in a certain way. Experimentation is clearly a method for increasing the likelihood of the prediction being correct.

Let us take a simple example of this. If you were to observe a dog drinking water, you would be likely to say that the dog was thirsty, inferring from past experience that a dog lapping up water has been deprived of water and is thirsty. This is a probable inference and in all likelihood a pretty good guess. Although this explanation is the most probable account of his behavior, it is possible that other factors might have played a role. For example, a bee might have landed on his tongue, or some cayenne pepper; or perhaps he was after a piece of meat at the bottom of the bucket. These are all unlikely events in terms of frequency of occurrence, so we base our interpretation of the dog's behavior on past experience. However, if we wished to increase the probability of our explanation being the correct one, we would experiment. We might take the dog and keep him in an enclosure for forty-eight hours without water. At the end of that time, we could provide food and water and see how active his drinking behavior would be. Assuming that depriving him had produced a tissue need for water and increased the likelihood of drinking, we could now place more confidence in deprivation as a critical variable in drinking behavior. With this established, we could return to our earlier explanations of the dog's behavior with added information and confidence.

It must be kept in mind that there is always an element of uncertainty in a prediction. Scientists must always be seeking methods of improving the accuracy of their predictions. This is essentially what we mean when we talk about controlling events. It is interesting to note that in the area of prediction some people, who ordinarily accept such basic principles of science as accurate observation, description, and experiment, feel that we have entered into a never-never land. Sir Oliver Lodge, for example, has observed, "Though an astronomer can calculate the orbit of a planet or comet or even a meteor, although a physicist can deal with the structure of atoms, and a chemist with their possible combinations, neither a biologist nor any scientific man can calculate the orbit of a common fly." Now, with all respect to Sir Oliver, this is rather a nonsensical statement. Who can ever say it is impossible to accomplish something? Only a nearsighted or pessimistic person could assume that observations or measurements currently unavailable to us will always remain beyond our reach. A careful reading of Sir Oliver's high-sounding statement should bring to mind one question: Who has *tried* to calculate the orbit of a common fly?

I am certain that if one thought it important enough to have such a calculation, steps could be taken to try to measure it. Let us play for a moment with this speculation, because it is one that seems to hit at the center of some of the assumptions we have made. We assume that behavior is lawful; therefore, if we are true to our own beliefs, the orbit of a fly in, say, a cathedral should be understandable, provided we had sufficient information about the organism and the environment in which it is behaving. How would we proceed to get pertinent information to predict the orbit of this particular fly? Perhaps we might start with an examination of air currents in the cathedral. Suppose we were to divide the cathedral into a grid and, in making accurate observations and measurements, learn that at point B-6—which is thirty feet from the floor and twenty-five feet from the west wall—there is a strong draft that provides a considerable amount of resistance to any object caught in that coordinate. We might assume that a fly would be less likely to fly into a resistance area, which would be pushing against its flight, than one offering less of an obstacle. This may be completely wrong, but at least it may be the beginning of a calculation of an orbit. Upon further investigation it might appear that temperature changes are a critical variable. (Certainly this seems to be true in calculating the migration of birds or spawning behavior in salmon, which Sir Oliver might also have considered beyond the ken of the scientist.) In addition, there may be such organismic variables as the presence of lady flies, the strength of the fly, the length of time since its last meal, and others, which might prove relevant.

I certainly have no intention of plotting coordinates to test out the idea that it may be possible to predict the orbit of a fly in a cathedral, but I feel sure that if this should be seen as something of importance in science, someone could work out a means of making such a prediction. In this context we can simply offer our respects to Sir Oliver and proceed to ignore him.

So far I have touched upon the elements of observation, experimentation, and prediction as they relate to the scientific method and the ultimate goals of understanding, prediction, and control. (Although I have not spent much time on the problem of control itself, it should be apparent that once we are able successfully to predict events we have achieved a degree of control over them.) At the moment, I would like to go back to the other basic element in the beginnings of scientific research, one that, coupled with observation, underlies all science, whether descriptive or experimental. This is the factor of measurement.

Measurement in Science:
Classification and Quantification

In discussing the question of description in scientific methodology, I have used a number of examples covering such differing things as a virus, a dog, and a fly. There are, to be sure, different levels of description in science, ranging from description of cellular activity in a human being to description of this same person studying for an examination. Generally, the narrower the focus of activity, the easier it is to measure. For example, a scientist might be infinitely more accurate in describing electrical activity occurring in a person's cell membrane than in describing the complex of events associated with studying. There are enormously complicated problem areas, such as that of tensions that lead to war and to racial and religious prejudice, that we have been unable to solve. In large measure we have not been able to solve them because they cannot be effectively described. In viewing such significant problem areas I agree with B. J. Underwood, who has observed, "I would defend the proposition that research in psychology necessarily involves measurement, and that the rapidity with which research will embrace . . . significant behaviors depends upon our ability to break them down into relevant parts which can be measured" (140).

To be sure, there are problems and events that simply overwhelm our capacity to understand: hundreds of people committing suicide in a cult in Jonestown (Guyana), snipers shooting innocent people, terrorists indiscriminately bombing innocent people. No psychologist is going to pretend easy explanations exist for such events. Can one approach a complex subject such as terrorism and attempt a beginning of understanding? Perhaps one can, and perhaps one would do best by first trying to see if any differences or similarities exist among terrorist groups.

Augustus Norton offers just such a beginning, a classification of terrorist groups by assumed motivation in which there are three nominal groupings: nihilists, secessionists, and irredentists (100). *Nihilists* are the most dangerous in many ways—they see a world that is evil and seek to destroy it (or to destroy the persons they hold responsible for it). They hope (we assume) that out of the ashes of destruction something better will arise. The Red Brigade of Italy exemplifies this group. The *secessionists,* as the name implies, want to be separated from another entity, as, for example, the Basques from Spain or the Quebecois from Canada. Both these groups wish to preserve a national identity and to separate from the majority. In the past the French-Canadian Quebecois were more active as terrorists until political gains for them became apparent; the Basques continue to practice terrorism. The third group, the *irredentists,* wish to regain a lost identity or territory. *Irredentistas* were active in late nineteenth-century Italy in a campaign to recover all Italian-speaking districts under the control of other nations. Modern-day irredentists (the word derives from unre-deemed or unrecovered) use terrorist tactics to effect what they consider such a recovery. The Palestine Liberation Organiza-tion and the Irish Republican Army (which seeks to unite all Ireland) exemplify this group. Does it help to differentiate be-tween the Red Brigade and the PLO? Perhaps not. But, as Nor-ton suggests, it may help to see that all of these groups indis-criminately kill or hold hostages under a threat of death, using terrorism as *theatre,* as a dramatization of their cause to call world attention to their demands. A handful of terrorists holding American hostages in the U.S. Embassy in Teheran used the press and international television as its theatre. A small group of terrorists may intimidate an entire nation by such tactics, as seen in November 1973 when a group of Fedayeen terrorists held a Dutch KLM Air Lines plane with crew and passengers hostage to try and force the Dutch government to soften its policy of aid-ing Soviet Jews in escaping to Israel. These remarks are not in-tended to be an apologia for terrorism but simply an illustra-tion, an attempt to understand the "incomprehensible." If a taxonomy of terrorists can help in understanding and controll-ing them, it would be a large step forward.

Naming and Weighing: Nominal and Ordinal. The two basic questions in measurement are: (1) *Does the phenomenon exist?* and (2) If so, *to what extent does it exist?* In scientific terms, the first question represents a *nominal* type of measure-ment. As the term "nominal" suggests, this is a naming oper-ation, which simply differentiates one event from another. It is a frequent basis of measurement description; for example, clas-sification of flowers or birds is a nominal operation. But let us see where this might lead.

Numbering prisoners in a penitentiary could be called a nominal measurement. This basic classification ("prisoner") may be sufficient for the needs of the prison authorities, but it is possible that they may wish to separate the prisoners into groups based on an estimate of the severity of the crime for which they were imprisoned. Assuming that forgery is a less serious crime than murder, prisoner No. 400-097 (a forger) is placed in a different cell block from that of prisoner No. 400-789 (a murderer). The numbers differentiate the two on a nominal scale; the separation in terms of severity of crime differentiates them on an *ordinal* scale. It is apparent that an ordinal scale—such as a rating of the severity of criminal acts—can be highly subjective. Suppose it were possible to work out an exact scale of severity in which the interval murder–forgery was equal in severity to the interval forgery–shoplifting. In terms of increasing seriousness of crime the ordinal scale would read: shoplifting–forgery–murder. If such a scale worked, it might be used by a judge in determining sentences or by a parole board in assessing release of prisoners. When an ordinal scale is divided into equal steps or gradations of such degrees of intensity, it is referred to as an *equal-interval* scale.

Another development in working out a scale is one in which it is possible to establish an absolute-zero point on the scale. An equal-interval scale with an absolute-zero point is called a *ratio scale*.

Physical Referents and Models. At this point I would like to express an opinion that may well meet with some disagreement. I would say that ultimately all measurements must have some physical referent (see Chapters 6–7). There are phenomena that are called subjective, but if they cannot eventually lead to measurement they cannot be considered as scientific data. This is not to make a shrine out of the methods and techniques used by physics and the other natural sciences, but to indicate that until subjective phenomena are rendered measurable and quantifiable they can yield little meaningful information. I believe that research problems such as anxiety and emotion—which have always been matters of concern for psychologists—may be most fruitful when approached in terms of physiological change and measurement of such physiological change. As we will see in Chapter 6, there have been many definitions of emotion; but the one factor common to all these definitions is some change in the activity of the autonomic nervous system—a physiological event that is subject to measurement. Covert behavior—which has often been referred to as unconscious and presumably not subject to experimental investigation—has in fact been studied in a careful and ingenious fashion by Ralph Hefferline and his colleagues (78). There are clear indications of the possibility of measuring minute behavioral events with physiological recordings.

We have seen that the information available to scientists is largely dependent upon the refinement of their instruments. Each year, as finer and finer instruments are made available to the researcher, more and more information previously considered subjective comes under the scrutiny of the experimental investigation.

Physical Models: Temperature and Time. One of the ways measurement begins is through the use of physical or mathematical representations of objects or events. We have come to accept a thermometer as a reliable indication of gradations of temperature, just as we have come to accept a clock as reliable. To illustrate the use of physical models as a means of establishing quantified measurement, let me first refresh your memory as to the origins of the thermometer, the ever-present and reliable measurement device.

Before the seventeenth century a nominal type of measurement was considered sufficient for evaluating cold and warmth. It seemed sufficient to say that something was hot or cold, or to use some very gross ordinal scale of ordering by saying, "It is colder" or "It is warmer." As Isaac Asimov (5) has observed, "to subject temperature to quantitative measure, it was first necessary to find some measurable change that seemed to take place uniformly with change in temperature. One such change was found in the fact that substances expand when warmed and contract when cooled." He goes on to discuss the research of Galileo, who, in 1603, first tried to make use of the fact that substances expand when warmed and contract when cooled by inserting a tube of air which had been heated into a bowl of water. As the air contained in the tube began to cool to the temperature of the room, it contracted and drew water up into the tube, thus creating the first thermometer. When the temperature of the room changed, the level of water in the tube also changed. "If the room warmed, the air in the tube expanded and pushed the water level down; if it grew cooler, the water contracted and the water level moved up. The only trouble was that the basin of water into which the tube had been inserted was open to the air and the air pressure kept changing. That also shoved the water level up and down, independently of temperature, confusing the results" (5).

As Asimov notes (5), the Grand Duke of Tuscany in 1654 worked out a thermometer that was independent of air pressure, containing a liquid sealed into a bulb to which was attached a straight tube. "The contraction and the expansion of the liquid itself was used as the indication of temperature change. Liquids change their volume with temperature much less than gases do, but by using a sizeable reservoir of liquid and a filled bulb, so that the liquid could expand only up a very narrow tube, the rise and fall within that tube, for even tiny volume changes, could be made considerable." Boyle did a similar experiment at about the same time as did the Grand Duke and showed that the human body maintains a constant temperature, which is much higher than the usual room temperature.

Water and alcohol were the first liquids used in the creation of thermometers, but water tended to freeze and alcohol boiled away. So the French physicist Amontons tried mercury. In Amontons's thermometer, as in Galileo's, the expansion and contraction of air produced a rise or fall in the level of the mercury. It was in 1714 that Fahrenheit combined the work of the Grand Duke and Amontons by enclosing mercury in a tube and using its expansion and contraction with temperature change as the indicator. Moreover, Fahrenheit made the contribution of putting a graded scale on his mercury tube so that the temperature might be read quantitatively. No one is quite sure as to the method by which Fahrenheit arrived at the particular scale he used on his thermometer. One account has it that he simply set zero at the lowest temperature he could obtain in his laboratory by mixing salt and melting ice, then setting the freezing point of clear water at 32° and its boiling point at 212°. Though this appears somewhat arbitrary, it was effective because it was maintained consistently.

In 1742 Celsius, a Swedish astronomer, adopted a different scale. As it was finally developed, the freezing point of water was set at zero and its boiling point at 100°, rather than the 32° and 212° of Fahrenheit. Because the scale was divided into a hundred gradations, it has been called the "centigrade" scale. The difference between the Fahrenheit and centrigrade scales has continued to plague students trying to remember whether it is 5/9(F°) − 32 or 9/5(F°) + 32 from Fahrenheit to centigrade. Because the centigrade scale (or, as it is known among many scientists, the Celsius scale) is more convenient, fitting in with the metrical system, it is used more widely among scientists, although the Fahrenheit scale is the most popular in the United States in nonscientific measurements of temperature.*

Referring back to our original notes about models, a thermometer, no matter what scale of temperature may be used, represents a physical model of contraction and expansion of a physical entity and is a reflection of changes in the environment. (Later on, in Chapter 6, I will talk a bit more about the use of physical operations in the process of definition.) At the moment I would like to comment on one more physical model that is used as a means of measurement in our approach to ordering the data of our world. This is the clock, a device that attempts to duplicate the apparent rhythmic movement of the sun. From this fundamental model of movement, the change in position of a clock's hands are taken to signify a passage of time designated by such terms as seconds, minutes, and hours. In a broad sense, it may be possible to begin a consideration of

---

* The recent introduction of the metric system into the U.S. has caused some concern, which is strange in a way, inasmuch as film has been metric for a long time (16 mm, 35 mm).

time by the nominal scale—such as the binary division of day/night, late/early, and so on—moving then to gradations of lateness or earliness or dayness or nightness. The gradations then are marked off in terms of units of time, ultimately duplicating the measurements inherent in the apparent movement of the sun.

Not all models are intended to be such clearcut physical duplications of other physical operations. When one talks of the brain as a computer or of a computer as a giant brain, all that is intended is to illustrate the similarity in the information-storing and -retrieval processes going on in brains and computers. Nevertheless, whether it be by analogue, model, or in the form of a conceptual system, ultimately measurement must have a base in a physical operation or it becomes pure sophistry.

And Psychology?

We have discussed models and the need for physical referents in measurement. How does this apply to the field of psychology? No matter what the particular interest or field a psychologist pursues—whether clinical, experimental, child, or physiological psychology—the basic datum with which psychologists deal is *change.* Clinicians are interested in how a person changes in therapy, a learning experimenter uses the datum of change in assessing learning, and so on. If change is indeed the basic datum for measurement in psychology, how then can it have a physical referent? By *action criteria,* which can be specific, precisely described behaviors in therapy; by objective, quantified learning measures; by accurately measured physiological changes. Let us take an example. A patient is given a drug in treatment. Before treatment the patient is in a particular physical state, which we call "Steady State A." The drug, called the "treatment," is administered. The next sequential state is post-treatment, "Steady State B." Measurement must be taken at at Steady State A, which is experimentally referred to as *baseline behavior,* from which comparisons may be made. Measurement must subsequently be made at Steady State B to see what changes occurred, presumably as a result of the treatment. This is of course slightly oversimplified, inasmuch as measurement will be made at many different times. But the important concept here is measurement as an objective index of change.

And here we sometimes run into problems. The individual who administers the drug will necessarily specify precise aspects of the drug administration. Let us say the drug is tetracycline, the route of administration is by mouth, and the frequency with which the drug is administered is four times per day. This would be, in medical shorthand: "tetracycline 250 mg, po, q.i.d." What is the problem here? There may not be as much care and specificity in documenting change after the drug has been administered.

Throughout this book I have criticized the use of vague terms such as "improvement" to characterize change. It is imperative, if psychology is to advance scientifically, that measurement be in terms of action criteria, of defined behaviors. The measurement of change has been described in psychology, in many contexts, as *performance;* performance can be seen as action. For example, even in so complex a matter as a phobic response in a patient, rather than speak of the individual "improving" (which is probably based on verbalizations rather than action criteria), the therapist may define a specific behavior to represent progress. Let us say the patient has a phobia regarding elevators. Desensitizing a patient for such a phobia, as Wolpe has done (148,149), involves systematic programming of specific behaviors, resulting in a final performance of riding an elevator. Here both the therapist's procedures and the patient's performance are clearly delineated. (The term "therapeutic contract" has been used to describe the expected behaviors on the part of both the therapist and patient.)

Because psychology is basically concerned with change, measurement in psychology is understandably a large area of discussion. The brief notes jotted down here reflect only one view, but one which I consider essential to scientific psychological measurement.

5

Two Fundamental Methods of Research: The Formal Theoretical and the Informal Theoretical

It is time now to consider the use (and nonuse) of theory in research. So far we have touched upon methodology and have skirted around the problems of the formation and testing of hypotheses.

By far the predominant methodology in science is the formal theoretical approach, involving the techniques of observation (an empirical one), hypothesis formulation and testing (through experimentation), and theory construction, leading to laws. Most people equate scientific method with such an approach. There is, however, another school of thought, which holds that data, not hypotheses, are the stuff of science and, moreover, that theory construction need not stand in the way of investigation.

Let us take each of these approaches in turn, first the traditional theory-construction method, then the informal theoretical, while recognizing that no matter what methodological differences may appear on the surface, the goals of science remain description, explanation, prediction, and control.

Data, Hypothesis, Theory, and Law:
The Formal Theoretical Method

Basic to scientific method is observation; all research begins with it. A researcher observes an event, wonders about it, formulates some tentative ideas about it, and sets out to test the accuracy of his ideas. These are the main elements: observation–hypothesis–experiment–verification. Students of theory construction characteristically use three different sets of operations, or propositions, in evaluating theory. These are

1. *empirical propositions,* which are statements of fact, what the observer has seen;
2. *hypothetical propositions,* which are statements of conjecture (based on the observer's empirical proposition, an hypothesis is formulated to account for the observed event to be tested in experiment); and
3. *theoretical propositions,* which are statements of the functional relationships among variables.

Melvin Marx has observed:

It is the hypothetical type of verbal proposition that forms the link between the empirical propositions, or facts, and the theories. The implications of a theory can be tested only by means of scientific predictions, or experimental hypotheses. These are questions which must be answered empirically. The hypothesis is thus the backbone of all scientific-theory construction; without it confirmation or rejection of theories would be impossible. Establishment of empirical propositions is referred to as *inductive* in contrast with the complementary development of the logical implications of theories, or the *deductive* phase of scientific investigation. (98)

Roughly, this may be limned as follows:

Observation   Empirical observation of *facts,* reported events

Hypothesis   Statement of *prediction* (if X is done, then Y should result)

Experiment   Test through *manipulation* of variables

     ↓

Results   Confirmation or refutation of hypothesis

     ↓

Theory   Statement of functional relationships among
                      variables

The theoretical framework now becomes a reference for future empirical observations, hypotheses, and so forth, with theory kept as a living body of knowledge and conjecture, subject to continual modification.

It is apparent that this system is not very different from other types of decision making or problem solving. An ordinary person making a decision or solving a problem tries to get as much information as possible (in computer language, he "scans"), evaluates this information in terms of the present situation and his past experiences (memory), decides on a course of action in which he makes a prediction (or hypothesis) that one course of action will be better than another, and, following the action, verifies his hypothesis (12). The final operation is one of storing this experience for future reference in a feedback to memory (13; see the figure opposite).

Clark Hull has suggested four essentials for a sound scientific theory (81), which may be restated and modified as follows:

1. *Definitions and postulates.* These must be stated in an unambiguous manner, so as to be consistent with each other or of such a nature as to permit rigorous deductions.
2. *Deductions* from these postulates must be made with meticulous care, exhibited for checking in full detail. Gaps in the deductive process lead to faulty theory.
3. The significant theorems of a scientific system must take the form of *specific statements* of the outcome of concrete experiments or observations. These predictions of outcome allow a test of the theoretical system, as we have seen in the preceding section on characteristics of theory.
4. *Carefully controlled experiments* must be devised to test the theorems deduced.

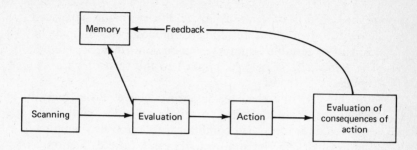

Hull sums up his position by observing that "scientific theory in its best sense consists of the *strict logical deduction* from *definite postulates* of what should be *observed* under *specified conditions*. If the deductions are lacking or logically invalid, there is no theory; if the deductions involve *conditions of observation* which are *impossible of attainment,* the theory is *metaphysical* rather than scientific; . . . if the deduced phenomenon is *not observed* when the *conditions are fulfilled,* the theory is false." (Italics mine.)

Hull's position is that the nature of scientific theory demands the observational determination of its truth or falsity. Truth he defines as a theoretical deduction that has been verified by observation, including rigorous experimentation.

Hull has described metaphysical theory as involving conditions of observation that are impossible of attainment. Following this thought, we may suggest the following schema:

Metaphysics: involves conditions of observation impossible of attainment. Theory demands logic and consistency but no experimental test. Religious questions would be included in this; belief in a particular body of religious ideas involves faith—acceptance of logic and consistency in the system. In general, no need is experienced for experimental proof, nor is such proof possible.

Pre-science: involves deducations that are capable of being stated in terms that permit experimental verification, though no experimental tests may have yet been accomplished. Much of psychoanalytic theory might be placed here; the deductions resulting from observations may be phrased in testable hypotheses to be confirmed or refuted. The same criteria may be applied to the field of parapsychology.

Science: involves the elements described above. Strict logical deductions from definite postulates of what should be observed under specified conditions, followed by manipulation through experimental test, rejecting false deductions.

Anatol Rapoport has given some criteria for testing a theory (108). I have modified and enlarged upon them.

1. *The problem of definition.* Can the concepts and definitions proposed in a theory be expressed so that they may be clearly communicated to others with operational exactness?

2. *The problem of reality.* Can the effects of an event be checked by others and shown not to vary under specific circumstances, to be stable and invariant?

3. *The problem of verification.* Can the assertions made about an event be verified by experience and be subject to accurate prediction? Is the assertion true?

4. *The problem of deduction.* Does the assertion made about an event appear logical and consistent within itself and with other assertions assumed to be valid, though not directly experienced? Is the assertion valid?

5. *The problem of causality.* Why did the event occur? (This is one of the fundamental questions posed.)

6. *The problem of communication.* Can the events and theoretical concepts be described in language (or other symbolic form) which will be clear and nonambiguous to the receiver of the information? (This is related to Question 1.) In other words, does the terminology or other formal structure used involve vague, mutually understood but not clearly defined communication, or operationally meaningful communication?

7. *The problem of parsimony.* Are the explanations economical in terms of the events described? "Occam's razor"* demanded that explanations be no more involved than those that will most economically explain an event, being certain to cover all questions. In psychology it is usually called the principle of economy, in which the simplest available explanation is to be preferred.

8. *The problem of relevance.* Are assertions made about events pertinent to the whole? For example, can statements made about particular events be used to explain general behavior? As an illustration of this question, could the assertions of a person talking of people in Las Vegas, Nevada, apply to all Americans? The problem of relevance is simply to determine which specific assertions are relevant to one group and which are applicable to larger wholes.

There are several points to be made about this standard theoretical orientation in science. Theory is a reasonable stage between hypothesis, experimental results, and the formulation of laws. A theory is a working model, which should be continually subjected to modification. A major objection to theory is that it may become a crystallized body of information or belief that in itself becomes the standard for evaluating new data.** In this sense, theory becomes metaphysical, and science can ill afford theories that outlast their utility as model systems. A theory begins to dominate data when a scientist becomes concerned with proving his theory to be correct at the expense of investigating the data, which may or may not support it. As Ernest Renan observed more than a century ago: "Orthodox people have as a rule very little *scientific honesty.* They do not *investigate,* they try to *prove* that this must necessarily be so. The result has been given to them beforehand; this result is

---

* My colleague Clifton Bailey refers to a computer as "Occam's Electric Razor."

** A good theory should be able to use data that fail to confirm hypotheses, simply by modifying the theory in the light of such data.

true, undoubtedly true. Science has no business with it, science starts from doubt without knowing whither it is going, and gives itself up bound hand and foot to criticism which leads it wheresoever it lists" (111).

A theory that becomes rigid is obviously not a good theory. But it is not uncommon for people to defend or attack a theory vigorously using the same data to support conflicting interpretations.* This is all right as long as the data prevail and the theories remain flexible. But what happens when a theory dictates observation, when expectations of what should be in a situation override actual observations? Here is an example of this, taken from Anna Freud writing about a psychoanalytic case: This was the case of a girl "in the latency period, who had succeeded in so completely repressing her envy of her little brother's penis—an affect by which her life was entirely dominated—that even in analysis it was exceptionally difficult to detect any traces of it" (67). Now *there* is an interesting observation. It was *"exceptionally difficult to detect any traces of it,"* but theory dictated that it *should* have been there. Therefore—the answer—she *"had succeeded in so completely repressing"* it, it could hardly be seen. This strikes me as a *bête noire* of theory. You cannot use the same road map every place you travel.

An interesting view of the development of a science comes from Thomas Kuhn, who uses the term *paradigm* to sum up significant changes in scientific theory and method (88). A paradigm for Kuhn is a scientific model that has two major characteristics. First, it offers a system by which events in the

---

* In this regard it is interesting to see two investigators talking about emotion. Magda Arnold in discussing recent theories of emotion says, "The yield of the last quarter of a century has been comparatively meager. During these years a great deal of effort has been devoted to experimentation and clinical research without much concern for integrating or explaining the data" (3). Too much data, not enough theory. Joseph Brady has observed, however, "In probably no other domain of psychological science has so little empirical data provided the occasion for so much theoretical speculation as in the general area of the 'emotions' " (29). Too much theory, not enough data. For the record, I agree with Brady.

field can be explained better than by existing models (such as Newton's *Principia*), thereby attracting a new group of adherents. Second, it is "sufficiently open-ended to leave all sorts of problems for the redefined group of practitioners to resolve." The paradigm becomes, rather than an object for replication, a model "for further articulation and speculation under new and more stringent conditions" (90). Thus the paradigm brings together a group committed to investigating it, to reevaluating existing theory and method, and to defending their findings. The group of investigators coheres in mutual experimentation. Kuhn strongly believes that the paradigm as a scientific revolution is the route to normal science, although the existence of too many models to explain events in a particular field where "competing schools . . . question each other's aims and standards" does slow scientific progress. To be sure, a science that is less mature than other sciences is more likely to have such competing schools; not long ago in psychology Hullians, Tolmanians, Skinnerians, Freudians, and others were identified as subspecies of psychologists. The lack of many competing schools in a science contributes to an emphasis on method as opposed to theoretical position that must be staunchly defended. Kuhn underscores methodological questions when he discusses *defining* "science," an endeavor he considers a waste of time and energy. A more reasonable question, he says, is: "Why does my field fail to move ahead in the way that, say, physics does? What changes in technique or method or ideology would enable it to do so?" (91). For Kuhn another question involving a methodological empahsis is: Does a science make progress because it is a science, or does it become a science because it has made progress? How many paradigms have fallen into disuse because they did not work or because newer methodologies created new paradigms?

On pp. 151–3 we discuss resistance to change among scientists. This sort of resistance is a normal response—and necessary, unless it becomes so rigid as to prevent new looks at events. To defend existing paradigms or models in scientific enterprise is to require the proponent of a new model to demonstrate its superiority over existing models. A paradigm may meet resistance, lie fallow for a period of time, and then be rediscovered. An example of this is the model advanced by a cancer researcher a number of years ago of a paradigm for cancer based on a virological model. A virus as a factor in cancerous growth of tissue did not fit in with existing data and theory at the time; the explanation did not offer enough to require investigators to consider it as a revolutionary alternative. It was largely as a result of data coming in from other fields that a possible virological model to explain cancer was reconsidered, decades after it was first stated. As a paradigm it is now a model to cohere an experimental group performing mutual study to garner the needed facts.

Kuhn also makes the point that science advances not as smooth "cumulation," but in somewhat erratic ways. Its advance depends in large measure, as we shall see, on a variety of disciplines and on the development of ever more sophisticated methods of obtaining data and handling data analysis. Revolution and reorganization are the dominant events.

Data, *Hypothesitos,* Order, and Law: The Informal Theoretical Method

Adhering to the second general method of research, the informal theoretical, is a group of investigators who believe that theory construction is an uneconomical way to do research and that researchers need only proceed from their observations to experimentation, then to some ordering of data to seek functional relationships among the variables, and finally to some formulation of organized law. Theories for this group are unnecessary because they are too formalized. These investigators consider that ordering the data and finding lawful relationships among them is the task of science, and fear that theories become solidified and begin to determine research rather than integrate reseach data.

Hypothesis testing is also considered to be uneconomical because the investigator working with a rigorous hypothesis feels obliged to follow it relentlessly, despite Skinner's unformalized principle of science that "when you run onto something interesting, drop everything else and study it" (123). The diligent pursuit of an hypothesis is considered by the informal theorists to be acceptable and good practice only if it does not keep you from seeing data as they begin to emerge. This group will willingly change an experiment in the middle if a new (and perhaps more promising) lead develops. They also suggest that there is no such thing as a negative result or a refutation of an hypothesis. To pursue this a bit further, investigators (such as Skinner) say that it is not good research technique to specify an hypothesis which will be confirmed or refuted. If one were to do this, they say, the confirmation of the hypothesis would provide a positive result, whereas the refutation would provide a negative result. They say that there is no such thing as a negative result, because any finding in an experiment is important if it provides information. Only by structuring an hypothesis in a rigorous, rigid fashion can a concept of negative results even appear. As Sidman notes, "When one simply asks a question of nature, the answer is always positive" (116).

The group of investigators who do not commit themselves to hypotheses may find some satisfaction in a famous quotation from Newton, *"Hypotheses non fingo"* ("I do not make hypotheses"). When Newton said this he meant that he derived his laws solely from observation of nature, which he thought was a process to be distinguished from formulating an hypothesis regarding the possible cause of the event observed. He also said, "I do not deal in conjectures." He believed that a careful, accurate observation of events in nature and a step-by-step pursuit* of these events would ultimately provide the material out of which a theory would evolve. A theory for Newton, and for us as well, would be some systematic formulation of the relationships among events. It is, of course, not entirely true that

---

* An interesting and amusing illustration of the step-by-step development of an experiment may be found in Skinner's "Case History in Scientific Method," which appeared in 1956 (123).

Newton did not make hypotheses. What he actually did was to wonder about the causal relationships among the events he observed. His hypotheses were created on the spot, as it were, without the general rigorous formulation of the hypothetico-deductive method. I think all investigators make these on-the-spot hypotheses. Some call them hunches; I choose to call them *hypothesitos,* which is semi-Spanish for "little hypotheses."

Another key principle of the informal theoretical group is the almost exclusive reliance on careful investigation of the single case rather than a large group of subjects. It has been traditional over the last hundred years to collect large numbers of subjects in order to obtain what is generally referred to as a representative sample, or a sufficiently large group from which to make general hypotheses. In using such a group approach, it is necessary to remember that the individual tends to become somewhat obscured; all the individuals are lumped together in a statistical entity that has no real existence. For example, you may speak of the interest pattern of the adolescent as though there were *an* adolescent representative of all members of such a group (reminiscent of the Platonic "idea of a class," such as a chair that represents the concept of a chair). All you are doing is pooling the most frequently encountered interests (such as sports, perhaps) of a particular group and noting that the average adolescent has this cluster of interests. This tells you little or nothing of a particular adolescent who lives across the street from you, except what you might possibly expect to find. Only an investigation of the individual can tell you whether or not his interest pattern conforms or deviates from the average. Then, if you wish to relate his performance to the group from if which he is drawn, you may place him as having other than average adolescent interests, meaning that he deviates from the norm to some degree.

Perhaps a more specific illustration may be drawn from the height distribution of a group. For example, a high school senior class has an average height of 5'8'', meaning that roughly two-thirds of the class cluster around that mean. This does not make a boy of 5' any taller or a boy of 6' any shorter. It might be important to know the average height for such a purpose as planning a procession; if, however, you wanted to order caps and gowns for the class it would obviously be necessary to take each individual's measurement.

In considering the importance of concentrating on the individual, Sidman, in a discussion of Skinner, comments,

> Skinner's rejection of "confidence level statistics" derives from his clearly stated interest in the behavior of the individual. This interest dictates an experimental design different from that generally used in psychology. Instead of running groups of animals and averaging their data, it becomes necessary to run individual animals through all of the experimental manipulations. Each animal thus constitutes a replication of the experiment, which not only affords an opportunity for detecting differences among animals, but also actually imposes the obligation to report them and, where possible, to *explain* them. The procedure of treating differences among animals as lawful, rather than as examples of the capriciousness of nature or of the experimental techniques, provides Skinner with one of his substitutes for statistical treatment. Experimentation is continued until the variables responsible for deviant behavior are identified. A corollary of this point of view is that any behavioral effect repeatedly demonstrated in the same animal is a lawful phenomenon. (122)

Sidman believes that the control of data in research does not depend on the amassing of large groups of subjects or even large samples from an individual subject. He states, "We must consider our science immeasurably enriched each time someone brings another sample of behavior under precise experimental control" (118). He believes that the adequacy of a technique in experimental psychology should be evaluated in terms of the reliability and precision of the control it achieves. This does not necessarily mean that apparatus (as an extension of human operations) is the answer. Apparatus only performs what the human sets up. A human experimenter can count the number of times a pigeon pecks at a key, but human accuracy is dubious in view of the rapidity with which a pigeon can peck—up to fifteen times a second. It is more accurate and simpler to attach a switch to the key so that each time the pigeon pecks he closes a circuit and puts a pulse into a counter that records the rapid pecking. Obviously this can be extended to ink-writer recorders, timers, and other pieces of equipment for various purposes.

The critical question is the type of data desired and the precision of control achieved. Here again is that word "control." By control, in an experimental context, we mean no more than the assurance that providing specific stimuli under precise conditions will result in a high probability that certain responses will be emitted by the organism. So, for example, in a simple T-maze experiment we would construct the maze so that the animal would have to run in one of two directions at the end of the maze, either to the right or to the left, with, perhaps, food in one arm of the T and water in the other. The determination as to which stimulus is more reinforcing or rewarding to the animal is made on the basis of a free-running animal's choice.

A more complex type of experimental control is found in experiments of the type reported by Skinner in which pigeons deprived of full feeding were placed in an experimental enclosure and left there for a short period each day (129). Every fifteen seconds, no matter what the bird was doing, a hopper containing food appeared for a few seconds, making food available. The environmental event began to exercise control over the bird's behavior. Despite the fact that the appearance of the food was clearly independent of the bird's behavior, certain well-defined stereotyped responses began to appear. If the bird happened to be performing some act, such as tossing its head, at the moment the hopper appeared with food, it tended to repeat the response. These responses included such unusual behavior between each hopper appearance as turning counterclockwise in the box two or three times and swinging the head and body like a pendulum. Because the response of the bird in this experiment bore no causal relationship to the appearance of the food but nonetheless persisted, Skinner refers to this type of response as a "superstitious" response. The incidental reinforcement controlled the behavior.

In this experimental situation the superstitious response increased in frequency and probability of recurrence because it was followed by reinforcing consequences (the hopper) even though the response in actuality had no causal relation with the reinforcement. In another kind of experimental situation, the behavior might actually produce the reinforcement, but under conditions that were in fact irrelevant. An experiment reported by Skinner and Morse illustrates this point (131). Pigeons were trained to a variable-interval schedule of thirty minutes, which meant that on an average of every half-hour a food hopper would be available to them. "Average" here means that an unpredictable series of reinforcements would occur—a reinforcement might be followed by another three minutes later, then by none for forty minutes; the thirty minutes was an average interval over the entire experimental period. The pigeons were trained to peck at a translucent key behind which an orange light appeared. For a period of four minutes out of each hour, at an unpredictable time, an incidental stimulus appeared—the light changed color from orange to blue. Occasionally, the blue light's appearance might accidentally occur at the same time that food appeared. If this happened, there might develop a type of *sensory* superstitious response in which a stimulus adventitiously (accidentally) associated with a food reinforcement took on properties of behavioral control. In the experiment reported by Skinner and Morse, one bird lowered its response rate in the presence of a blue light; another raised its pecking response (131). In either situation the bird responded to the appearance of an incidental stimulus that had no causal relationship to the food reward as though it actually did affect the food reward, which is a reasonable definition of superstitious behavior.

How is it superstitious to respond to a stimulus event in this manner? Let's take a human example. First, the unpredictability of the appearance of the food on the variable-interval schedule in the Skinner and Morse experiment tended to produce a stability of responding. Such a schedule of reinforcement accomplishes a response rate that has a steady pattern. This organism is unable to tell when the reinforcement of the food hopper will appear and therefore continues to respond in a steady fashion to avoid missing a reinforcement.

From anthropological studies of magic and ritual comes a statement from Malinowski that seems relevant to the experiments described above.

> An interesting and crucial test is provided by fishing in the Trobriand Islands and its magic. While in the villages on the inner Lagoon fishing is done in an easy and absolutely reliable manner by the method of poisoning, yielding abundant results without danger and uncertainty, there are on the shores of the open sea dangerous modes of fishing and also certain types in which the yield varies greatly according to whether shoals of fish appear beforehand or not. It is most significant that in the Lagoon fishing, where man can rely completely upon his knowledge and skill, magic does not exist, while in the open-sea fishing, full of danger and uncertainty, there is extensive magical ritual to secure safety and good results. (96)

Here Malinowski is contrasting an unpredictable condition, dangerous open-sea fishing, with a predictable lagoon in which fishing is done in an "easy and reliable manner." Where uncertainty exists, magic and ritual—superstitious behavior—occur; where predictability rules, no such superstitious behavior is found. Thus, the control by the environment of specific behaviors is illustrated by the pigeon work, in which adventitious reinforcement and incidental stimuli set the occasion for behaviors, and by the Trobriand Islands observations, in which the conditions attendant upon important food-seeking behavior controlled responding. In Malinowski's situation, magical ritual could be viewed as a response pattern associated with the behavior of the individual or the group at the time of the rein-forcement's appearance.

In a like manner, neurotic behavior can be viewed as super-stitious in that the individual goes through certain behaviors as though they were causally related to events. Mild neurotic superstitious behaviors occur in all of us: the Naval Academy student who rubs Tecumseh's bronze nose for luck, the tennis player who always wears a certain color for luck—you can fill in your own examples. True neurotic behavior in a disturbed individual can often demonstrate superstitious behavior. For example, in a case reported by Harold Lief (94), a woman caught her husband in a compromising position with another woman and, among other responses, threw out the dress she was wearing at the time of the incident because it upset her. When she learned the "other woman" worked at a particular drug store, she emptied her cabinet of all drugs bearing the label of that drug store. Eventually she presented herself for treatment because she could not drive her car. The reason for her inability to drive was that she would become upset upon entering a road she knew would lead her by the drug store or by the motel in which her husband's affair took place. Lief refers to this case as "sensory association of phobic objects," in which accidental events (wearing a particular dress) occur-ring simultaneously with a traumatic event, take on phobic, superstitious qualities. Here, the dress was an incidental stimu-lus, the aversion to the dress a superstitious association. The interested student would find the case rewarding; a more de-tailed discussion may be found in Bachrach (9).

A final note about superstition: Do you really believe it is all that unusual? Take a skyscraper. Think of the engineering; the metallurgy; the mathematics; the knowledge of stresses of concrete, metal, and glass; the architectural precision needed to produce a draftsman's blueprints for the construction crew. Given all this engineering and science, is it not a bit astonishing to find that the thirteenth floor was omitted?

Control occurs in many circumstances in the environment. Try looking often at your watch when a friend is talking to you and observe his speech rate—does he speed up to finish what he wants to say or does he slow up, hesitating in view of your clock-watching? This is a rudimentary form of control. Look at stimulus control. You are in room A and you need something in room B, so you go to room B and find you have forgotten what it was you went to get. So you go back to Room A, where the object is *not* located but where the stimuli that evoked your searching behavior *are*. Perhaps you stand there until you get hit with the evoking stimulus again. Stimulus control is an important environmental event in maintaining our behavior.

I have gone on perhaps overlong in providing examples of control. I have tried to demonstrate that we are under control by the environment or individuals within it—parents, friends, lovers, teachers—all of the time. It is the means by which we influence each other. Experimental control is, again, the establishment of environmental circumstances (stimulus conditions) of a precise nature to set the occasion for a response by the individual. By programming consequences (contingencies, reinforcements) the experimenter hopes to control the response by influencing its frequency or perhaps its intensity. In other words, by setting up a consequence of responding, the control aims at influencing the probability of that response recurring. There is really nothing very magical about the word "control."

Control of the experiment and the data is essential in any methodology—formal theoretical or informal theoretical—and steps must be taken to insure such control. I have referred to some of them in this chapter. In the next chapter I am going to take up the crucial problem of definition. There is a need to specify the variables with which the experimenter is working. Definition of terms is a basic means of control.

CHAPTER

6

The Problem of Definition

We have seen in our earlier discussions that measurement is basic to the scientific method and that measurement itself is of two fundamental types. First, the nominal type that asks the question, "Does the phenomenon exist?" and second, the type of measurement that asks the question, "If the phenomenon exists, to what extent does it exist; what is its magnitude or intensity?" In order to be able to formulate some sort of measurement for a phenomenon, one must define it clearly and unequivocally. This brings us to one of the basic problems of the scientific method: the definition of the variables, phenomena, and events with which the scientist is concerned.

On the surface, this might seem like a relatively simple problem, since our daily life is so filled with naming and defining objects. But it is in just this deceptive simplicity that the real problem of definition lies. We are so accustomed to dictionary definitions that we tend to think of these as being clear, unequivocal, and real. At this point I would observe that a major error in scientific method is the uncritical transfer of dictionary definitions to scientific method, for dictionary definitions do not define in a scientific manner.

The main problem with dictionary definitions is, as Robert Graves and Alan Hodge observe, that "English dictionaries are ctions of precedents, rather than official code-books of ɹeaning'' (71). Accordingly, dictionaries do not—can not—keep up with current meaning. This is not all bad, however. It is highly unlikely that a word such as "rush" will have any dictionary definition other than something like "a charge in football" for a long time to come. Nor, as *Esquire* magazine notes in "The-Out-Of-It Alphabet," will such words as "uppers" and "hung" (103). The linguistic aspect of this is noted by Skinner.

> Theories of meaning usually deal with corresponding arrays of words and things. How do the linguistic entities on one side correspond with the things or events which are their meanings on the other side, and what is the nature of the relation between them called "reference"? Dictionaries seem, at first blush, to support the notion of such arrays. But dictionaries do not give meanings; at best they give words having the same meanings. (103)

Ultimately, there must be some clear operation to which these words may be related.

Ideally, the referent (or referents) should be physical, and agreed upon by observers in defining the object. The optimal description is triangular: the tangible object, the observer, and the defining word.

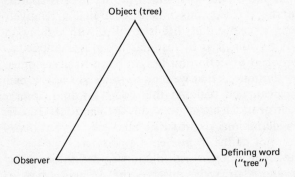

Object (tree)

Observer

Defining word ("tree")

It is not until we get into more abstract kinds of defining words that we get into operational problems. Moving from "tree" (physical) to "truth" (abstract) is not only a large philosophical jump but a tremendous semantic leap as well.

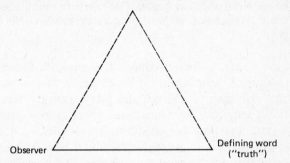

Observer

Defining word ("truth")

Many years ago Stuart Chase, in a book entitled *The Tyranny of Words,* suggested a useful technique. He suggested that "abstract words and phrases without discoverable referents would register a semantic blank, noises without meaning." As an example (45), he drew upon a political speech by the aspiring Hitler:

> The Aryan Fatherland, which has nursed the souls of heroes, calls upon you for the supreme sacrifice which you, in whom flows heroic blood, will not fail, and which will echo forever down the corridors of history.

What Chase suggests is that every time you come across a word that does not have a clear physical referent, you simply substitute "blab." Thus he translates the Hitlerian speech as:

> The blab blab, which has nursed the blabs of blabs, calls upon you for the blab blab which you, in whom flows blab blood, will not fail, and which will echo blab down the blabs of blab. (46)

This is a technique that might well be applied to most commencement addresses, political speeches, and much professorial

comment. With regard to the latter, Chase also gives an illustrative example:

> Education implies teaching. Teaching implies knowl-
> edge. Knowledge is truth. The truth is everywhere the
> same. Hence education should be everywhere the same.
> (47)

Here the writer, a famous educator, starts with four high-order
abstractions: "education," "teaching," "knowledge," and
"truth." He then establishes absolute identity: "Knowledge is
truth." Then, as Chase observes, there is one truth for all
places and presumably for all times. While we may have a
vague general idea of what this means, it would be impossible,
in practical terms, to plan a curriculum for a real school with
real children on the basis of something that we must take for
granted as having an abstract and indeed comforting intellectual sound.

Three Levels of Definition

To pursue the problem of definition a bit further, let me suggest that there are three levels of definition, which I call *daily,
poetic,* and *scientific.* The daily definition is one that is universally accepted and for which there is a general understanding.
The poetic definition need not be universally accepted or generally understood, but is treated as belonging within the realm of
individual license and creativity. The scientific definition is
restricted to a limited group for which the definition must have
specific meaning. To take an example, suppose we define "the
moon" from the standpoint of daily, poetic, and scientific
communication. The daily definition might be: "a round, heav-
enly body that revolves around the earth and reflects the sun's
light and becomes full once a month." The poetic definition
might be something along these lines: "a silver crescent, glow-
ingly set against the velvet blackness of the brooding sky." Finally, a scientific definition might be something like: "a heav-

enly body, a satellite of the planet Earth (the third planet in the system of Sol) that revolves around the planet once every twenty-eight days, has a mean distance from the earth of approximately 238,000 miles and a diameter of approximately 2,160 miles, and reflects the light of the sun (Sol)."

It might be noted that an accurate definition of the moon from a scientific standpoint must inevitably define such things as planet and the system of Sol (which is a Type GO star) and so on. The three types of definition obviously differ in their clarity and their specificity. As I have mentioned, a major error is the transference of a daily definition (or, less likely, a poetic one) to scientific usage. An astronomer could hardly perform meaningful scientific measurements using concepts that would be acceptable in daily conversation, such as "becoming full once a month." The scientific definition must deal with specific and unequivocal description. It might also be observed at this point that the transfer of scientific communication to the daily or poetic realm would be equally inappropriate. The lover at a lakeside who describes the moon to his sweetheart as the satellite of the third planet, Earth, in the system of Sol, would probably be as unsuccessful as a poetic astronomer at a scientific meeting. In daily conversation such descriptions are considered pedantic.

There is another crucial factor that differentiates daily, poetic, and scientific definitions and approaches. This is the matter of *belief*. When a person communicates in daily matters using daily criteria, hyperbole is not uncommon: "I have a million things to do before Friday." This is an acceptable, if literally unbelievable, communication. In the poetic realm, suspension of belief may be an essential part of the communication. Certainly, even a person who thoroughly rejects the possibility that ghosts exist is not going to walk out in a huff when Shakespeare has Hamlet dealing with the ghost of his father. Is it not also true that we accept the cartoon possibility that a dog can run a good distance off a cliff into empty air and not fall until he "realizes" he is without support? Such suspensions of belief in the poetic realm have been called by Walt Disney the "plausible impossible." In poetry and in daily communication they are acceptable. In scientific communication no such suspension of belief is possible; we must believe that the scientist is communicating fact.

The Problem of Clarity

It cannot be overemphasized that a major error in applications of the scientific method is the use of daily definitions. This is a very frequent problem in certain types of research, especially those dealing with human behavior and clinical problems. For example, take the word "anxiety"—a common word for which there is a fairly clear daily definition. Even a word like "personality," which has a large number of meanings,* is relatively clearly understood in certain contexts, even though these usages differ. For example, personality is something that one can have ("He has a lot of personality"). That one can talk about "a lot of" suggests that there is some rough scale of magnitude going from a little to a lot. It is something that can be treated with a value judgment ("I don't like his personality"). It designates certain identifying characteristics, as in "He is a Hollywood personality." These are all daily definitions that have relative clarity within the specific usages for which they are designed. Like the word "anxiety," the word "personality" leads to confusion when scientific research is attempted. To talk about a "personality disorder" suggests that something is disturbed, but what? Only by rendering a vague daily term such as "personality" meaningful and subject to scientific definition can any significant research be attempted.

Certainly textbooks are not the final arbiters of definition, as may be seen in the following definition of anxiety from a standard textbook in psychiatry: "Anxiety, in a sense, is the

---

* Probably it has too many meanings, or "surplus meanings," in Hans Reichenbach's sense (110). Marx has commented on this in observing that concepts with surplus meanings may be "tolerated in the early prescientific development of a field but their replacement by constructs more closely and necessarily tied to the data must occur for scientific advance" (98). This is the major point with which we deal in this chapter.

ego's warning mechanism that something is awry within the personality. The ego itself uses anxiety to indicate that either something within the id or something in the super-ego threatens the ego" (60). While there may be some general understanding of such a statement, it is apparent that scientific understanding could never emerge from it. In order to make such a definition meaningful, "ego," "superego," "personality," "id," and "anxiety" itself must be defined in clear and unequivocal terms, ultimately to be related to observed, demonstrable, and repeatable events tied to the data.

There is a touch of circularity in any such case in which the entity to be defined becomes part of the definition. Skinner, as we have noted, has indicated that dictionaries do not give true definitions or meanings of a word, but generally give other words that have the same meaning. In an involuted definition there is a loss of clarity; so in addition to the book definition of anxiety, we find definitions of depression—such as "heightened sadness" or "feelings of despair"—that simply tell us that depression is depression.

Related to this problem is Bertrand Russell's theory of types, which says that an entity cannot be used to define itself. To illustrate this he proposed a square as follows:

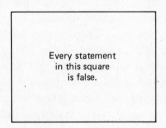

Every statement
in this square
is false.

If the statement is true, then it is obviously false. If the statement is false, it is patently true. The proposition that a statement whose terms are properly defined cannot logically be both true and false is known in epistemology as the Law of the Excluded Middle.

I mentioned earlier that a definition of the moon might ultimately require further definitions of "planets" and "satellites" and other terms used in a scientific definition. But this kind of definition is different from that required for terms such as "id," "ego," and "personality." The former kind (defining the moon) may be related to observable and demonstrable events, while "personality," "id," and "ego" always remain formal verbal symbols. I will touch upon this again as we continue our discussion.

One phase of this problem of definition may be summed up by a quotation from Willard Quine, who observed, "The less a science has advanced the more its terminology tends to rest upon an uncritical assumption of mutual understanding" (107). When individuals communicate observations with mutually understood but vague terms (such as "personality") instead of with terms based on scientific grounds, research is retarded. To bring up another example, if one were to go through research dealing with psychotherapy—loosely defined as "the treatment of emotional problems"—one would come upon the term "improvement" used widely to indicate a change in the person's behavior. Yet rarely is there any clear definition of what is meant by improvement. If you were to ask a psychotherapist what she meant by improvement, she might say, "Well, everyone knows what improvement means," just as she might say, "Everyone knows what anxiety means" or "Everyone knows what personality means." This is the use of the mutually understood, universally accepted, daily definition in a situation that demands scientific definition. To say that "everyone knows" is to beg the question and avoid the major issue of clarity and certainty of definition. The mutual assumption of understanding, as Quine has suggested, is indeed an immature approach to scientific method.

An Attempt at Clarity and Certainty: The Operational Definition

What have we to offer in the way of a meaningful scientific definition? Fundamental to all scientific method is the *opera-*

tional definition. While there are problems with regard to the operational definition, by and large it is clear that scientific method depends upon it. It is defined by Anatol Rapoport in the following terms: "An operational definition tells *what to do* to experience the thing defined. Asked to define the coefficient of friction, a physicist says something like this: 'If a block of some material is dragged horizontally over a surface, the force necessary to drag it will, within limits, be proportional to the weight of the block. Thus the ratio of the dragging force to the weight is a constant quantity. This quantity is the coefficient of friction between the two surfaces.' The physicist defines the terms by telling *how to proceed* and *what to observe"* (109). The operational definition of a dish, it has been suggested, is its recipe.

In scientific method, we need to have items that may be operationally defined, although it is undoubtedly true that the very nature of the language itself may preclude complete operationalism. The important thing is to emphasize the necessity for approaching this goal by eliminating the mutually understood but vague terms (in Quine's sense) that impede adequate communication.

In the past I criticized the American Psychiatric Association's *Diagnostic and Statistical Manual: Mental Disorders* for its classification of the "chronic brain syndrome," which read as follows: "The chronic organic brain syndromes result from relatively permanent, more or less irreversible diffuse impairment of cerebral tissue function" (58). This "description" appeared in a manual published in 1952. Subsequent manuals have improved the operational meaning of the definition and have eliminated "relatively permanent" and "more or less irreversible," which were operationally unsound. (Thank you, but I really don't believe I had anything to do with the change.)

Nomenclature—which is a nominal classification of events, species, disorders, or anything that can be labelled precisely—is necessarily based on operational criteria.

Recall where the term "nomenclature" came from originally. It started with the *nomen clator,* a servant employed by a

Roman gentleman to walk in front of him and call out the names of approaching individuals. This service was very helpful, inasmuch as it freed the gentleman from having to remember the names of all the citizenry whom he approached. The *nomen clator* would call out the name Publius Ovidius Naso, enabling the gentleman to greet him properly. If the *nomen clator* had said, "It's *probably* Publius Ovidius Naso" or "I'm *pretty sure* it's Publius Ovidius Naso," his nomenclature, and probably his position, would have been in considerable jeopardy.

It is apparent that the operational definition starts with observation. The observer records and reports facts and tries to communicate these in a manner that will give maximal clarity. One of the objections to maximal clarity is that the number of definitions involved may become exceptionally cumbersome; the closer one approaches certainty and clarity, the more specific and particular one becomes, while science itself must ultimately lead to generality and prediction. I do not believe that this is a legitimate objection to the use of operational definition. I think that the number of definitions required depends upon the specific circumstance.

Percy Bridgman has suggested that common usage prefers ambiguity and a small number of words to clarity and a great number of words (30). But this is not entirely true. For example, in our own particular culture there is one word for snow, and while we may give qualifying characteristics to this—such as hard, soft, crusty, or slushy—common usage does indeed prefer ambiguity to a large number of words describing snow. In the Eskimo culture, however, in which one's life and livelihood depend upon a precise knowledge of the type of snow, there are reported to be thirty words to describe different kinds of snow, each one having a different form. Clyde Kluckhohn has observed that different cultures may emphasize different areas, just as the Eskimo emphasizes discriminating descriptions of snow. He notes that English "is very discriminating about flocking behavior: we speak of schools of fish, herds of cattle, flocks of sheep, coveys of quail, prides of lions, etc." (86). We can only assume that a culture that develops discrimination about flocking has a need for such discriminations, while other cultures appear satisfied with indicating only that there are "many" sheep or cattle. I confess I cannot comprehend the need for such fine differentiations.

James Lipton, in his charming book, *An Exaltation of Larks* (95), tells us more about groupings and other linguistic aspects. "Exaltation" was indeed once used to describe a group of larks, just as "a doctrine" grouped doctors—both uncommon, but uncommonly colorful. A further discrimination, based on class lines, is offered by Lipton from the novel *Sir Nigel,* written by Sir Arthur Conan Doyle, creator of Sherlock Holmes. In this novel, young Nigel comes under the tutelage of Sir John Buttesthorn, who asks Nigel what a group of boars would be called. Nigel replies,

> "One says a singular of boars."
> "And if they be swine?"
> "Surely it is herd of swine."
> "Nay, nay, lad, it is indeed sad to see how little you know. . . . No man of gentle birth would speak of a herd of swine; that is the peasant speech. If you drive them it is a herd. If you hunt them it is other."

The "other" for the gentleman hunter is a "sounder of swine."

A single word may be used in many different contexts provided there is clear operational specificity for each use. For example, the word "key" has over twenty meanings in English, each one related to a specific operational referent (music, fraternity, house, and so on). Perhaps this could also be done with greater operational clarity for the many-sided word "personality."

It has been done, in a rudimentary sort of factor analysis, by a group of psychologists who tried to find some consistent meaning in the word "emotion," for which they found over twenty definitions (147). When these psychologists factored out the element common to all the definitions of emotion, they found one characteristic appearing in all: altered activity of the autonomic nervous system. It is obvious that a layman's definition of emotion would not be apt to bring in that particular phrase, but his description of the behavior involved would probably indicate an increase in heart rate or perspiration, or something similar in physiological activity. These are altered activities of the autonomic nervous system and go along with descriptions couched in more professional terms. When a factor can be pinpointed, this gives us the beginning of a more satisfactory definition of a word such as "emotion." We have something that is measurable (and you know how fond I am of things that are measurable).

The context of—or stimuli that evoked—the altered physiological state is crucial to defining the emotion. For example, suppose you are sitting in class when the door bursts open and a young man runs in. His face is red and slightly perspiring, he is breathing rapidly and somewhat erratically, his movements are quick and excited. He could be in a rage, or very scared, or perhaps sexually aroused by the girl who was climbing the stairs before him. To define the emotional state is to determine the situation that aroused it—exercising a certain amount of caution, of course.

Observation always must start with specific, clear, and restricted definition. Only on this basis can there be any movement toward a correlation of specific observations, making for a more general body of knowledge.

A frequent objection to operational definitions is that they ultimately push the definer into a corner. Rapoport has commented on this with an amusing illustration in which he points out that a strict logical positivist, using his principles and standing by them completely, could not say, " 'There is a black sheep.' He could only say, 'I see a sheep, one side of which is black.' If asked whether he did not really believe it was a black sheep, he might say, 'My previous experiences with sheep whose one side was black lead me to expect that if the sheep turned around, I should receive similar sense data' " (108). This description may appear ludicrous, since the observer sounds overly compulsive in his description. But if one were to substitute the word "moon" for "sheep," it becomes a different matter. Until recent space penetration and exploration an observer could only say, "There is the moon, one side of which has craters," because no one had seen the other side of the moon and experience limited us to conjecture about the other side. In other words, we have seen many sides of sheep and have the experience that allows us to infer (with a high degree of probability) that a sheep will be the same color on both sides. While there was certainly a good degree of probability that the other side of the moon would have craters, there was no experience that allowed us to make such an inference. The operational definition or logical positivist description of the moon had to be restricted to a description of what was currently observed.

Another objection to operational definition that has occasionally been raised is that it is possible to give operational definition to symbolic entities, and therefore the definition is robbed of operational clarity. This is not really a significant problem, inasmuch as science always deals with two types of propositions, which have been described as *formal* and *empirical*. S. S. Stevens, for example, in discussing the operational method has observed that "hypotheses . . . can be only formal statements —operationally empty—until they are demonstrated" (135). In clarifying this, he makes a distinction between formal and empirical propositions, saying that formal propositions are symbolic and have no empirical reference. "They are language, mathematics, and logic *as such.*" For example, it is possible to state in a formal proposition that $X = a + b^2$ without any reference to the objects or events described by X, a, or b.

Empirical propositions, on the other hand, are "those in which these arrays of symbols have been identified with observable events." Rapoport has described this also in terms of a propositional function, noting that the propositional function allows a hypothetical statement to be made, such as *"X is green"* (109). It is impossible to tell from this formal statement whether it is true or false. If X is grass, there is demonstrable truth; if X is milk, it may be considered false. Mathematical symbols, as a whole, need no immediate empirical reference but may exist within a purely formal structure.

Formal symbols may appear in operational definitions, as in the following example. A psychologist is describing the conditions under which he performed a certain experiment and notes in defining "hunger" (a subjective daily definition that he attempts to render operational): "The rats in this experiment were deprived of food for a period of seventy-two hours" (an accepted procedure for rendering an animal hungry). The word "hour" is a formal symbolic word that has a relationship to, but is removed from a purely physical event. We have discussed this earlier (pp. 57–8) in considering levels of measurement, but a brief recapitulation of the principle in this different area may be of some help. The psychologist uses the term "hour," a nonphysical, verbal, formal symbol that has come to be the sign designating a specific passage of time indicated by the movement of a pair of hands around the face of a clock. The movement of the hands is a physical operation that has been given symbolic designations ("second," "minute," "hour"). The final physical operation is the movement inside the clock itself that produces the movement of the hands. A clock is a physical model of the apparent rhythmic motion of the sun. Thus, when a psychologist says he has deprived a rat of food for seventy-two hours (thereby defining hunger), he is using a verbal symbolic definition related to two other levels of definition of movement—both physical—signifying passage of time and the clock model. He need not go into this when making his statement, because it is known.

The critical point made by this illustration is that verbal, symbolic definitions or terms may be used provided that there are some data to which they can be related and these data are physical operations. Defining anxiety, in the example given earlier, in terms of egos, ids, and personality merely compounds the problem because there is never any physical operation to which these purely formal, verbal symbols can be related.

Inferred and Invented Concepts

Decidedly related to the above is the question of *inferred* and *invented concepts*. It is obvious that many of the concepts with which the scientist works are inferred from data and that others are constructed to account for certain observed events. For example, the nucleus of an atom is an inferred concept that has its origin in observed data and presumably exists in a real sense. The discovery or observation of the nucleus itself will depend upon the development of finer and finer measurements. And so, while the term "nucleus" may have formal properties and be differentially related to physical events, ultimately it may itself be a physically observed event. The term "hypothetical construct" has been used to describe this type of inferred concept, presumed to exist and for which it is expected that experience will provide later disclosure.

In contrast to the hypothetical construct or inferred concept, there is the invented concept (referred to frequently as an "intervening variable") used by the experimenter to account for events that he has observed. Heredity and learning are such intervening variables. Neither heredity nor learning may be seen in a physical sense, but they are nonetheless operationally defined as invented concepts. To illustrate this further, heredity is an intervening variable that has been invented to account for certain observed physical events. At one point in history, the gene and chromosome were hypothetical constructs that were inferred as mechanisms of the transmission of heredity. Genes and chromosomes have physical reality and as such can be disclosed. Heredity is not a physical event but a concept created to account for physical operations. Similarly, learning is an intervening variable; but a change in the neurophysiological structure of the brain, which may be inferred to occur in learning, has not been clearly isolated and remains an hypothetical construct. But it is rooted in data and is presumed to exist as a physical operation. Further research may yield more information.

To sum up our discussion of operational methods, I would like to turn to Herbert Feigl (63), who has set up the following criteria for operational methods, which I have modified:

1. They should be logically consistent, that is, derived logically one from the other and be related to other operational definitions.

2. They should be definite, preferably quantitative.
3. They should be empirically based, linked to the observable.
4. They should be technically possible, subject to experimental manipulation.
5. They should be intersubjective and repeatable, demonstrable in different species and repeatable by different experimenters.
6. They should aim at the creation of concepts that will allow for laws or theories of greater predictiveness.

It is obvious from the above that Feigl's concept of operational methodology is clearly related to our previous discussion of theory and its construction, dealing with logically derived, consistent terminology for data that are measurable, based on observation, subject to manipulation for testing, repeatable from subject to subject and experimenter to experimenter, and, finally, aimed at the creation of some order of cohesion of facts into a system.

One often hears the cliché that nature has all the answers available and it is up to the experimenter to find the right question to pose. There is a great deal of truth in this, and I would suggest that it is only through the use of clarity in operational definition of one's variables that the right questions may be posed.

It is, I am certain, apparent that the operational definition involves more work for the individual doing the defining. It is a lot easier to be less precise, but not as scientifically satisfactory in the long run. Let me leave you with a classic example of the comforts obtained by casual definition. It is from Lewis Carroll's "The Hunting of the Snark":

> He had brought a large map representing the sea
>   Without the least vestige of land:
> And the crew were much pleased when they found it to be
>   A map they could all understand.
>
> What's the good of Mercator's North Poles and Equators
>   Tropics, Zones and Meridian Lines?
> So the Bellman would cry: and the crew would reply
>   "They are merely conventional signs!"

CHAPTER
7

The Laboratory and the "Real World": Animal and Human Research

In Chapter 3, we noted that there are psychologists, in particular the humanistic psychologists, who do not believe that results found in the laboratory—often with lower organisms such as white rats—have much relevance or applicability to practical problems of the everyday, human world. In fact, other researchers and practitioners of psychology think the highly controlled conditions under which research is accomplished may create an artificial situation from which it is difficult to generalize.

For example, in a long, intensive series of laboratory experiments simulating the isolation and confinement encountered in space flight and undersea habitat dwelling, subjects (Navy personnel) were placed in isolation chambers where they lived and worked together for periods of up to ten days. In many of the conditions, the experimenters found that team members began to express hostility toward each other, even to the point of an attempted stabbing. Mannerisms tolerated under nonisolation conditions became highly irritating; some of the experiments had to be terminated because of the danger of bodily harm. These were well designed experiments; skilled researchers, using TV, tape recording, and sophisticated measuring devices, analyzed them. But the problems in simulated settings did not materialize in the actual space or undersea environments where men were isolated and confined. The generalization of the problems encountered in the laboratory situation to the real isolation situation never occurred. And here lies the problem of all types of simulation—in the experiments, no real threat to life existed. The sailors in the experiment knew that if anything were to go wrong, there were many people on the other side of the locked door to let them out.

Not so in actual space or undersea. The astronauts orbiting in space could not elect to terminate the experience, nor could Houston Space Control simply unlock a hatch. The men living undersea in SEALAB II, 205 feet below the ocean surface off the California shore, were under increased atmospheric pressure and dared not surface without the decompression required to reabsorb the gas bubbles in the body resulting from pressure (105). (Without such decompression, a probably fatal case of decompression sickness—known as "the bends"—or an air embolism might occur.) The obvious difference between the simulated experience and the real world was that in the latter there was real danger to life. The men counted on each other for support, and they could not simply ask to be let out; therefore, they were obliged to adjust to the environment. In fact, divers in SEALAB II who did not get along well on the surface took pains to work well together on the ocean bottom: As one diver said, "We were walking on eggs!"

Does this mean that the laboratory isolation experiments were useless? Not at all; they revealed many interesting data about human behavior under those stress-simulation conditions as well as important information about stimulus-deprivation and limitation. Also important is the lesson learned, that simulation must be generalized carefully to the real world.

Egon Brunswik's concept of the "representative design" is germane here (38). Briefly, a representative design characterizes an experiment that has a minimum of artificiality and a maximum of control. It is an ideal design in that it brings the problems of the "real world" together with the exact methods of the experimental laboratory. As may be seen in the following figure, an ideal experiment is one at the point where reality and control cross, but as so often happens with ideals, most experiments fall short of perfection. This does not mean that the ideal criterion should be overlooked. Some compromise is always experienced in applying laboratory methods to larger problems, but this is, as we have seen (pp. 48-9), part of the methodology of science by which the experimenter, through controlled procedures, attempts to establish the probability that a particular explanation is correct.

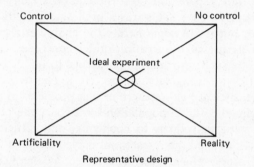

Representative design

There are times when laboratory experiments are not sufficient for answering certain questions, and the researcher necessarily takes his techniques and study procedures into the appropriate site of operation. For example, an important question for the armed services at the present time is how well women can perform duties in Army and Navy units. This is not an academic question; growing numbers of women have entered the services and increasingly have been assigned to previously male duties and roles. A laboratory experiment could not begin to assess how men and women would act toward one another in the field (literally), how they would perform their respective tasks, and how their interaction would affect the readiness of the unit to perform. One study (151) examined the effects of varying percentages of female soldiers assigned to combat support units. A total of forty companies—eight each from medi-

cal, maintenance, military police, transportation, and signal
sections—were selected. Although these were not combat
troops, their function was crucial in support of combat soldiers. The differences in performance between companies that
had changed from no female soldiers (0 percent) to 15 percent
female and those that had changed from 15 to 35 percent female were slight and not statistically significant. There was some
evidence that the former companies (0–15 percent) showed a
slight decrease in performance and the latter (15–35 percent)
showed a slight increase. Up to the percentages studied, women
soldiers did not impair unit performance on seventy-two-hour
intensive field exercises. This was a preliminary study that will
be repeated; but it did demonstrate the characteristics of field
research in its use of observation under controlled conditions
and its use of such information-gathering techniques as questionnaires (for assessing satisfaction, etc.). The study also had
the characteristics of field research in that problems of personnel
shift (changing the subject population somewhat), the lack of willingness of some individuals to cooperate, and difficulties with
weather that impaired the research all played a role in the study.

Related studies have been conducted at the U.S. Naval
Academy in Annapolis (150) and in an enlisted Navy school
population (80); these studies also were designed to answer the
question regarding male-female roles and performance. Field
research, largely, fits the reality aspect of the representative design with minimal artificiality, but clearly without the controls
possible in the laboratory. For answering certain questions it is
the only method available to the researcher.

Another type of field research—the survey—involves trying
to predict people's behavior. How does one predict whether a
new product will sell well or how a political candidate will fare?

Ideally, if one wished to find out what a particular city's
population said about a candidate at election time, one would
interview every citizen. The compromise with such an ideal is
rendered necessary by the impossibility of such a task; the time
alone required to interview, say, a million people, would be
prohibitive. So the pollster takes a *representative sample,* hoping

to slice out a segment of the population that represents a cross section of the whole, with enough workers, businessmen, professional people, and so forth to form a microcosm of the city. Whether or not the representative sample is successful is always a problem for poll-takers, but it is, nonetheless, illustrative of a laboratory procedure used in a real situation to establish probabilities of an event's occurrence, that is, the probability of one candidate emerging victorious. Based on his or her poll, the pollster establishes odds, i.e., by guessing at the outcome of the election—perhaps 55 percent for candidate A, 40 percent for candidate B, 5 percent undecided. The many factors that might play a part in shifting such odds are taken into consideration up to the last moment of the election. To be sure, poll taking represents an adaptation of the laboratory procedure of sampling, but it lacks the precision of the laboratory with regard to precise control of the variables after the selection of the subject population. This is, however, an excellent illustration of the way improved instrumentation results in improved data collection and analysis. The use of the high-speed computer, with its capability for storing enormous numbers of facts—population characteristics, previous voting records, and similar data in a community—coupled with its ability to integrate rapidly and analyze stored and new information, has enabled pollsters to develop infinitely greater degrees of accuracy in prediction.

A criticism often leveled at the laboratory is that it deals with trivial facts. As we have seen, the narrower a focus of activity is the easier it is to measure, and so the objection is heard that laboratory results are not solutions to problems, but only abstracted and unimportant facts. In psychology, for example, one might ask: Of what relevance to the protean problems of human behavior is it if a rat turns left in a maze or if a pigeon learns to discriminate between a circle and a square? But beyond any possible relevance to problems in human learning, there is still another consideration: Science progresses by accumulating unities among seemingly diverse and disparate facts. Thus it is by the discovery of what may appear to be superficially unimportant details that science builds its superstructure of theory. Perhaps most important of all, one discovery leads to another as one result points out another problem. Science is a regenerative discipline where one fact leads to other possible events in an ever-widening vortex of new information. As Bronowski has stated,

> I do not think that truth becomes more primitive if we pursue it to simpler facts. For no fact in the world is instant, infinitesimal and ultimate, a single mark. There are, I hold, no atomic facts; in the language of science every fact is a field. (34)

But Why Animals?

There still remains the question, But why animals? Assuming that students go into psychology as a career or sign up for a psychology course out of interest in human behavior, why do they get sidetracked into working with the ubiquitous white rat? And what does this have to do with human behavior? Skinner has discussed this question.

> We study the behavior of animals because it is simpler. Basic processes are revealed more easily and can be recorded over longer periods of time. Our observations are not complicated by the social relation between subject and experimenter. Conditions may be better controlled. We may arrange genetic histories to control certain variables and special life histories to control others—for example, if we are interested in how an organism learns to see, we can raise an animal in darkness until the experiment is begun. We are also able to control current circumstances to an extent not easily realized in human behavior—for example, we can vary states of deprivation over wide ranges. These are advantages which should not be dismissed on the *a priori* contention that human behavior is inevitably set apart as a separate field. . . . It would be rash to assert at this point that there is no essential difference between human behavior and the behavior of lower species; but

> until an attempt has been made to deal with both in the
> same terms, it would be equally rash to assert that
> there is. (128)

In the above quotation, Skinner illustrates some aspects of the use of animals in research, particularly the possibilities of doing certain kinds of experiments with animals that could not be conveniently performed on humans, thus yielding facts that can become increasingly relevant and important to human behavior. He also states a critical point germane to the question of the differences between animal and human behavior: We cannot be rash enough to assert similarities or differences until we have the data.

One reason, then, for animal research is the *feasibility* of conducting research with animals that could not be carried out on human subjects. Brain functioning, for example, is not as clearcut an area as some texts portray it to be in the interests of simplicity. Volumes have been written on such everyday events as sleep and consciousness without giving a truly clear definition of these events. Much of the work accomplished in the important study of brain functioning has been done on animals, in which areas of the brain have been removed, stimulated with electrical current, or subjected to chemical and surgical injury, all with an eye toward seeking out the answers to the structure and function of the brain and central nervous system. Could these experiments have been performed on humans? Obviously not. No systematic surgical ablation of or implantation of electrodes into the brain of a human subject to study such questions as the effect of electrical stimulation of brain centers would be permissible. Yet for the solution of such crucial questions as causes of epilepsy and other neurological diseases such as multiple sclerosis, such experiments—possible only on animals —must be performed.

The question of which animal to use in experimental work is another matter. Some experiments tend to dictate the species used. For example, rats lack color vision, and an experiment requiring color discrimination could not use rats as subjects.

Pigeons, on the other hand, have excellent vision, including color vision, and might be good subjects for such an experiment. Their exceptionally high rate of response in pecking at a key in an experimental box also has obvious advantages in an experiment requiring high rates of response. Monkeys and chimpanzees also have good response rates, and their advantages in size and similarity to humans in many respects make them important experimental animals. If one wished to use an animal whose behavior most closely resembles human behavior (partly by species characteristic and partly by close human contact), in all probability one would select the dog. (Does the name Pavlov ring a bell?) Cats, conversely, are notoriously recalcitrant experimental subjects in behavioral research.

Genetic studies of species with short life spans, allowing for many generations of study, can be done only with animals such as the fruit fly. It would be impossible for an experimenter to go through more than two or three generations of human beings himself in a genetic study, and it would also be impossible to manipulate genetic factors for study. This can be done with animals.

There are other reasons to choose particular animals as experimental subjects. L. K. Bustad suggests that the busy experimenter who has to leave town every once in a while to consult in Washington might wish to use the big brown bat. As Bustad notes:

> It weighs only 25 grams, doesn't eat much, and has minimal housing requirements. The big advantage is that, should one find that an absence of a month or two is suddenly necessary, this experimental subject may be placed in a cigar box with a supply of water and stored in a refrigerator. Upon returning from travel status, the investigator may retrieve his bat from the refrigerator and initiate his experiment after less than an hour's thawing time. This animal has been utilized in studies of micro-circulation and of the thyroid gland. (41)

He also suggests that the armadillo might be a good experimental animal. He has me interested here, as a researcher in underwater behavior and physiology, because the armadillo can hold its breath for ten minutes and incur a huge oxygen debt. Among the other advantages that Bustad notes is that the armadillo is hearty, "does not bite or kick," and will eat anything. The real advantage for a research worker is that "the female gives birth to monozygotic quadruplets." Thus the experimenter may remove one fetus of a quadruplet litter "at different stages of development without affecting the other fetuses. . . ." This possibility has an exciting research potential, for studies have shown that different litters of armadillos have differing characteristics. With a single uterine environment held under strict control, other relevant genetic and environmental variables may be studied most carefully.

Obviously, the animal chosen for a particular experiment, like the experimental methodology and the equipment, must be appropriate to the purpose of the experiment.

It is true that, with all the intellectual reasons for using certain experimental animals, a researcher may develop preferences for one species over another and find many of his experiments dictated by his favorite animal. I confess to being a pigeon man, and many of my experiments have been conducted with these birds as subjects.

One more caveat about the use of animals. In learning studies, the great majority of animal studies have been accomplished in controlled laboratory settings; subjects were from a limited number of species, primarily pigeons, primates, and the ubiquitous white rat. For the reasons previously discussed, these species are excellent laboratory animals, but one must also recognize that there are species-specific behaviors to be considered when restricted numbers and types of animals are used.

It also has been true that field research has contributed significantly to the body of knowledge in animal behavior. Earlier, we discussed naturalistic observation such as that practiced by

Goodall in her chimpanzee work. Most of the field research has been of this naturalistic type, with ethologists producing the greater volume of work (141). In more recent years experimenters have applied conditioning techniques of learning to study wild animals. For example, researchers have studied "bait shyness," a behavior long reported in hunting and fishing journals in which animals avoided bait. These investigators studied the effect of toxic agents in conditioning food aversion (74, 75). By treating food with lithium chloride and encasing it in hides—for example, treated mutton was put into sheep hides and treated dog food was put into rabbit hides—they conditioned wolves and coyotes to avoid live sheep and rabbits, although the bait had only flavor and textural stimuli with absolutely no physical resemblance to a live, intact animal. These studies of animals in the wild, experimentally controlled, have marked implications for learning theory. Learning occurred rapidly, even in one trial. It also occurred after a delay in time, because the illness occasioned by consuming the toxic bait did not affect the animal until long after eating; thus, there was no immediate contiguity in time of response and consequence. A final theoretical point of interest—generalization took place from one set of cues (the stimuli of the toxic bait) to the intact prey (the sheep and rabbits) and resulted in aversion. These experiments illustrate that laboratory principles and procedures in the all-important study of learning can be applied successfully to field research.

Students interested in research should avail themselves of every chance to work with different species in different kinds of experiments and let their own reinforcement histories (in terms of what they find most rewarding) lead them.

The Analogue Error

To return to Skinner's statement that it is too early to assert differences or similarities between animal and human behavior, let us now consider an important aspect of this question. Critics of extrapolations from animal to human behavior see a

gap that cannot be bridged between the behavior of animals
and human beings. However, those of us who see the relevance
of some animal work to human behavior often suggest that
there are more universals than may appear obvious. One example is found in programmed learning and teaching machines used
with human students, the basis for which is to be found in previous learning research using pigeons as subjects. With the need
for more experimentation in basic laws of learning, this problem may be at best academic, but one fact stands out clearly
and deserves attention: There is often an erroneous approach
to analogy between human and animal behavior that only leads
to further confusion. This analogue approach is based on the
assumption that to study a phenomenon in animals that is
related to human behavior it is necessary to set up a completely
analogous condition—for example, that to study psychotic behavior, we must render a rat psychotic. Let us consider the analogue error in greater detail because of its centrality to the
problem.

When a psychologist does work with animal subjects in an
experiment, someone might say, "This is all very interesting,
but what does it have to do with human behavior? It's nice that
you have been able to produce ulcers in white rats, but what
does that tell us about ulcers in people?" This is the heart of
the analogue error: the assumption that there must be a one-to-
one relationship between the two events. If we wish to study
disordered behavior in animals, it is erroneously assumed that
we must reproduce the same type of behavior disorder found in
humans. But, as Sidman observes, "Why should we expect a
rat's psychosis to bear any surface resemblance to that of a
human being?" (119). He goes on to suggest that a certain class
of factors may result in a human being's going to live in a cave
(in what the culture would consider a psychotic manner), while
the same class of factors in a rat may lead it to continue to
press a bar to get fed long after the food magazine has been
withdrawn. Our problem is not to create an analogue of human
psychotic behavior in the rat, but is, as Sidman further notes,
to obtain "sufficient understanding of both rats and men to be

able to recognize resemblances in behavioral processes. We must be able to classify our variables in such a manner that we can recognize similarities in their principles of operation, in spite of the fact that their physical specifications may be quite different'' (120).

Let me present a more detailed example of such an approach by taking a common human behavioral problem— depression. If you were to describe a person who is depressed, you might say, among other things, that he is listless, has lost his appetite, does not do much, looks sad, lies around the house or sits and stares at his feet, and talks in a low and monotonous voice (if he talks at all). All of these are behavioral descriptions which might fall under a general class of lowered activity and unresponsiveness. Suppose we were able to determine that an event was associated with this generalized unresponsiveness—for instance, the loss of his fiancée. The observer reports that the person received a letter from his girl breaking their engagement and then began to exhibit behavior similar to that described above. He would not eat, paid little attention to his friends, missed classes, spent much of his time lying in bed staring at the ceiling, and generally looked sad. We can say, in technical terminology, that a generalized reinforcer was withdrawn and appeared to be the occasion for the lowered responsiveness, or, as the others in the dormitory said, "His girl broke off with him and he's depressed."

It is manifestly impossible to reproduce those exact conditions in the laboratory—that is, to have a monkey receive a "Dear John" letter. But we can set up a study in which behavioral processes may be investigated that might have some relationship. Let us start with a model of the student's behavior: S will stand for stimulus and P for person, the student. The schema might be sketched as shown on page 105 (top figure).

S_1, his fiancée, has been removed, breaking the responsiveness to that particular type of stimulation. The effect of extinction (withdrawing the positive reinforcement or pleasurable consequences of the relationship) spreads to the other stimuli so that he becomes unresponsive to S_2, S_3, S_4, and S_n. (The

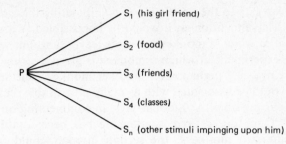

spread of effect of conditioning and extinction is well known in learning research.) So now we have the beginning of a model. We might elaborate on this a bit further and consider other aspects to study. Before the actual breakup of the engagement, it is possible that there were events that signalled a disturbance in the relationship between the student and his girl. Perhaps one day he saw her walking in the park with another man, holding hands. This would probably have been a disturbing event, a stimulus that might have warned him of impending unpleasant events. His behavior in the face of a warning stimulus such as this might have become agitated, upset, or angry. The letter informing him of the termination of their engagement followed upon such warning stimuli and may be considered the final unpleasant event that occasioned the depression. So we can add to our model by placing warning stimuli in the system: S_w (for warning stimulus) appears between the student and S_1 (his fiancee).

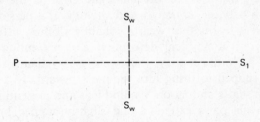

We can now take this model and see what behavioral processes in the lab may be established to study it, creating conditions appropriate to the problem and manipulating these conditions. As I have mentioned, it would be impossible to set up an experiment in which a monkey's fiancée leaves him, but we can set up an experiment in which a monkey is given a strong generalized reinforcer, perhaps even another monkey. The second monkey would be associated with as many pleasurable reinforcing events as possible. As Sidman says, in commenting on such a study, "Once the desired relationship has been established between the two monkeys, the second monkey could be removed, leaving the first one bereft of the source of many of its reinforcements. We could then observe any subsequent changes in the behavior of the experimental animal. We might even use a warning stimulus to signal the impending withdrawal of the generalized reinforcer and note the behavior of our monkey in the presence of this stimulus" (121).

The warning stimulus, for example, could be a red light that would go on before the second monkey was to be taken away. Do we have a depressed monkey in this case? It doesn't matter whether you call it that or not. If we can establish that there are similarities in the behavioral processes that go on in human and animal upon the removal of a strong rewarding stimulus, it doesn't matter what you call this process. The monkey may refuse to eat or it may gorge itself on bananas, the human may refuse food or turn to liquor. What we are interested in is the behavioral processes of both in the presence of similar conditions.

In sum, the crux of the analogue error is the failure to distinguish between *similarity* and *analogy*. If a person begging on the street learns that wearing shabby clothes, affecting (or really having) a physical deformity, and presenting a pitiful mien will get more money, then we may say that his behavior has been shaped to bring him the most reward. If a bear in a zoo learns that standing on his hind legs and presenting a front view with his paws extended and slightly cupped brings him more peanuts from visitors, we may say also that his behavior has been shaped to be the most rewarding. There is similarity—

a particular pattern of behavior is successful and is continued. We may say that both the shabbily dressed human and the standing bear are begging, but this may be anthropomorphically questioning the begging.

8

Ethics of Research: General Considerations

Ethics and Morality in Science

Long debates have occurred within scientific and philosophical circles regarding the ethical and moral characteristics of science. Robert Cohen is one scholar who views science as necessarily being ethically neutral and amoral. "We come to realize again that science is morally neutral. It has not automatically been a force for good. . . . Furthermore, the extension of science to the study of society and history is no guarantee of a humane commitment within the scientific community, nor of moral wisdom within scientific knowledge" (48). A scientist cannot allow questions of an ethical or moral nature to intrude upon his experimentation and methodology. If he has a question about the morality of his research, he should perhaps ask it at the beginning ("Shall I get into this area of experimentation?"—as with, let us say, bacteriological warfare) or after the experimentation is completed ("What applications will be made of my research?"—a question posed by the Archbishop of York to British scientists about the uses of the inventions they create; see p. 153). The experimentation itself is tactically determined and directed by scientific method, which is concerned with a different kind of ethical and moral problem, that of honesty and integrity. Stated otherwise, science does not concern itself with *values* during the course of research. But values themselves can be subjected to scientific study.

As M. W. Wartofsky suggests, there are three basic questions regarding the relation of science to value:

1. Is value amenable to scientific study, and may the object of such study be taken as either natural or as human, societal fact? Is there a science of value; that is, is there a rational, validated system by which value can be studied?
2. What values are exhibited *in* science and scientific method? Is there an *ethos* or ethics of science?
3. What is the value of science? What larger interest does science subserve or subvert? (144)

In our own scientific method, a major reason that neutrality or amorality exists is tactical. The prevailing scientific method in our culture, as we have seen earlier, is keyed to a probability of events. The concept of probability (p. 49) determines the structure of the experimental question: What are the chances that this event will occur, given certain experimental manipulations? Confidence-level statistics are geared to assessing such probabilities within a range of confidence statements; the odds are that this event will most certainly occur (a probability of 1.00). But probability, useful as it is in scientific method, also engenders certain philosophical consequences. It leads, for one thing, to a disbelief in absolutes; few things always or never occur (on multiple-choice examinations don't you tend to avoid choices that say "never" or "always"?). This disbelief strengthens a world view in which relativism is dominant, and this extends to ethical considerations as well.

The relativistic, probabilistic world view exerts a marked influence upon, and comes under the influence of, the culture in which it stands. Max Weber has pointed out that "the belief in the value of scientific truth is the product of certain cultures and is not a product of man's original nature" (145). To be sure, the reliance upon experimental method as a means toward 'the truth is, as we shall see, more characteristic of Western societies than of others and is clearly both a shaper and a product of the Puritan ethic, which believes in a rationalistic world order that can be discovered and altered (pp. 154–5). With a world view that sees events as less than absolute, it is possible to visualize change and ways of restructuring events. Cultural anthropology has contributed importantly to such a view. Florence Kluckhohn has described two world views that vary in their acceptance of the inevitability of absolutes—"man subjugated to nature" and "man versus nature (or *over* nature in the sense of rational mastery of it)" (87).

The scientific order based on the probabilistic, rationalistic view of the world provides its own ethics of science as a cultural phenomenon. Science and ethics become guides to rational action; as in a democratic society rational action involves an orchestration of the independence and interdependence of individuals, so it does in science. Cohen (48) has observed that "the ethics of science is the democratic state of a cooperative republic" in which citizens decide policy and ideas are tested with what William James once called a "robust sense of reality." The democratic ethic of science also allows for interdependence and respect. When an Einstein supplants a Newton, he does so not as a beachmaster replacing a vanquished sea lion but rather as a participant in the evolutionary process of discovery—that is, the act of supplanting is committed with the respect properly accorded an elder statesman.

Inevitably, the question of values or ethics in science focuses upon scientists themselves, as scientists and as citizens. They may condemn themselves if they allow value judgments to interfere with the execution of their research; they may also condemn themselves if they are not concerned with value judgments as citizens. Nowhere has this dilemma been more dramatically demonstrated than in the concern shown by nuclear physicists after World War II (see pp. 153–4) regarding the use of the nuclear energy they had developed. This group, referred to somewhat pejoratively by critics as the "League of Frightened Men" (a designation the men themselves agreed to), expressed its anxieties about the applications of atomic power. As scientists they had performed optimally; as humans and citizens they wished to perform equally well.

And, of course, the concern grows as nuclear energy is assessed as part of the worsening energy crisis. The emotion engendered by an accident such as the one at Three Mile Island is understandable. What is profoundly needed in such a situation is information, objectively obtained and accurately assessed. And this is the role the scientist should play in the circumstances. Press releases with preliminary information designed to soothe may further alarm; and premature alarms sounded, also without factual base, do not serve the all-important need of providing a sound basis for decision and appropriate action. Scientists, as objective observers and reporters, must concern themselves with information. If, after their scientific travails, they change clothes and participate as protesters against nuclear power in a demonstration, that is entirely their business and their right. But then they do so as citizens, expressing an opinion that, one hopes, is based on data sounder than the newspapers may have provided to the general public. There are times when this twofold desire to function as scientist and citizen may indeed prove a problem.

Our culture tends to exploit the universal expert. A person successful in one field, such as football, need not know any more about automobile batteries than the ordinary citizen, but he often influences ordinary citizens in their purchasing by endorsing various products. Scientists may not be as aware of social and political events as they are of experimental methodology, but as citizens they are morally bound to interact as best they can with their culture. Too often the scientist is not adequately prepared for the complexities that exist in the culture. For example, psychologists who sincerely wish to apply some of their knowledge to social problems often find that their knowledge of the community is sparse. The critical question of who really makes the decisions in a community ("Is it the Mayor?") can affect the most worthwhile endeavor. A colleague of mine who was interested in juvenile delinquency in a southwestern city found that the statistics of minor crime were contaminated because police officers merely reprimanded youths of a certain sociocultural status, yet booked those from lower levels of society, thus distorting the data on frequency and source of crime. In such a case, the psychologist interested in delinquency must first determine the accuracy of the community report. I sincerely believe that most of us are ill-equipped by training to make such a determination. The average first-year student of social work probably knows more about community organization than the majority of Ph.D.s in psychology.

The preceding paragraph may seem pessimistic. It is not intended to be. I wish to emphasize that the scientist who seeks to express a citizen's concern and to participate in the application of scientific knowledge to the solution of important community problems must be as rigorous and as well-equipped to take on such applications as he is to conduct his experimentation. Otherwise he is in danger of creating a large cadre of compassionate incompetents who mean well.

In sum, the ethics of science exists. It exists as a system of the rationalistic, industrious pursuit of facts. The choice of an area of research and the applications of the research accomplished are moral concerns for the scientist; the conduct of the research is not, except as it involves honesty and integrity of performance.

Biomedical Ethics: Some Lessons

Advances in technology and science often place new ethical concerns before the scientist. For example, in recent years the development of artificial kidneys and means of keeping heart activity going in patients who otherwise would have died, coupled with advances in organ transplants, have created ethical dilemmas for scientists. Consider the question, "How are we now to define death?" Electrical stimulation can keep a heart going, so the traditional definition of death as "heart stoppage" may not be appropriate. This realization has led in recent years to the reexamination and subsequent redefinition of death as irreversible cerebral stoppage. The brain then comes to be considered the center of life rather than the heart. Recent statements have clearly focused on neurological signs. For these, L. P. Ivan (82) and the Canadian Medical Association (43) suggest unreceptivity and unresponsivity of the patient to externally applied stimuli; no movements or breathing that can be detected (either spontaneous or evoked by pain, touch, sound, or light); no elicitable reflexes; and, finally, the flat electroencephalogram (EEG, or brain wave). Thus the definition of death becomes a matter of irreversible brain damage, with the assumption that, given artificial means of stimulating the heart or oxygenating blood through the tissues of the body, unless the individual is able to function on his own (through the mechanism of cerebral activity) to provide life support for such vital organs as the heart, he is functionally dead.

The prestigious Institute of Society, Ethics and the Life Sciences (known as the Hastings Center because of its upstate New York location) has supported a brain-death model, which has become the basis for several state laws on the definition of death (133). The theological and philosophical questions that are raised are complex and, indeed, far-reaching.

Other pressures create ethical dilemmas. What does a clinical practitioner do when, in the course of therapy, it appears that the patient under treatment admits to being the arsonist the police have been looking for in a series of fire-setting incidents? To whom does the psychiatrist or psychologist owe allegiance—the patient or society? Does the therapist look upon arson as another symptom of the patient's disordered behavior, strictly to be kept within the confidence of the therapeutic relationship, or assume a role responsible to the community and therefore report the patient to the authorities—perhaps preventing further incidents that threaten life and property? You will not find universal agreement on where the therapist's responsibility lies in circumstances of this kind.

Another pressure that has grown in recent years is that of the litigious nature of our society—the tendency for individuals to seek redress through lawsuits in increasing numbers. Malpractice, for example, is a problem the medical community would like to eliminate as much as the public. But the ethical question can be illustrated in a situation such as that of the physician who orders a highly extensive (and expensive) series of diagnostic tests on a patient, not because they are all needed but because of the risk of an eventual legal action in the event the patient is not satisfied with the physician's treatment. Why? Because the patient's attorney will undoubtedly ask the physician if, for example, a glucose tolerance test had been done; if the answer is "No, I didn't think it was needed," the physician is on the defensive. Thus many costly, unnecessary, and perhaps painful tests are administered so the physician can be covered.

Public Concern With Research

Returning to the ethical questions in research, there is no doubt that one of the thorniest problems faced by researchers is that of gaining maximal information about the subjects used in studies within a humane ethical framework. Research procedures have frequently been a source of concern and, indeed, alarm to the nonscientist. The layman's image of the scientist (which will be explored more thoroughly in Chapter 10) is usually not an accurate one. The most apparent misconceptions about science and the scientist are those concerning experimental procedures. Occasionally, scientists receive letters from people who have read about some research (usually in the newspapers) and who express strong concern about the procedures used. Often there is insufficient information given in the news-story to allow for adequate understanding of the purpose of the research, the techniques, and, in particular, the many humane safeguards taken to prevent unnecessary pain and discomfort to the animals used. An example of such a situation may be drawn from the experience of a colleague of mine who was working with the development of vision, a critical problem of great importance to human welfare and science. A woman read of the experiments, in which kittens were used because of the similarity of their visual development to humans and the feasibility of carrying out intensive studies of change in an animal that matures quickly. This woman, obviously a sincere animal lover, took the time to write a letter to the university in which this research was going on, protesting what she believed to be cruel and unnecessary practices in the laboratory. Her letter follows:

> I've learned of experiments on helpless kittens and cats perpetrated in laboratories of your University, financed by taxpayers' money. I feel sure you do not know about them.
>
> Contact lenses were put into the eyes of young, UNANESTHETICIZED kittens, and later the visual nerve cells in their brains were connected to microelectrodes, to compare them with cats who had had visual experience while growing up.
>
> Many people, some of them famous, have been wearing contact lenses very successfully a long time. SURELY, it was a cruel, USELESS WASTE of money, time and labor?
>
> Doubtless, there are many other cruel experiments going on at your University, a black stain on its fair name. WHAT is the effect on the character of the experimenters?

The newspaper story had been written with a high degree of accuracy, and there was, of course, human-interest value and some humor in a scientist grinding contact lenses for kittens. What was not clearly conveyed in the story was the general purpose of the experiments. The letter written in response to her letter tried to provide the needed background and information.

> We sincerely appreciate your concern about the animals used in the research and wish to assure you that under no circumstances do any of the animals suffer any pain whatever. The micro-electrodes you have read about which are used to study nerve cells are not a great deal different from the electroencephalographic

studies done on humans in hospitals to detect the presence of brain tumor or epilepsy. The purpose of the contact lenses, which do not even provide discomfort for the kittens, is not to see whether contact lenses are successful or not—certainly, as you indicate, they have been proved successful for quite some time. The purpose of using contact lenses is merely to control visual cues in a developing young animal to provide very critically needed information about the development of vision. Again, may I say that these cats are not uncomfortable, and certainly not in pain through the use of these contact lenses which are ground with precision by the very able researcher in charge of the project.

This kind of experiment is not cruel and certainly is not useless. We know very little about the development of vision and the kinds of experiments that Dr. _____ and others are conducting may provide extremely useful information about sight, hopefully to provide information which would help to correct visual defects and perhaps even to prevent serious defects such as blindness in children. One cannot use human subjects in these experiments largely because the development of the child is much slower than that of the kitten. The kitten, as you know, is fully grown in about a year, developed as an adult, hence the changes in visual acuity and different kinds of perception occur in a manner similar to the human, but at a much more rapid pace, and are more susceptible to careful study.

It is important for laymen to be sufficiently concerned about the welfare of animals and humans in research and to raise their voices in question (and in support). It is also important for them to have enough information to be able to question wisely. In this, the willingness of the scientist to communicate and the cooperation of news-media personnel and scientists —as we will see in Chapter 10—is an essential part of the communication of relevant and appropriate information.

CHAPTER

9

Ethics of Research:
Practices and Procedures

So far in our discussion of ethics the emphasis has been largely of an abstract sort, discussing value systems and ethical choices. When we turn to the all-important question of ethics in research, we leave the abstractions to deal with practices and procedures, the actions that must be taken or the procedures that will not be followed. Specific behaviors are necessarily involved.

Ethical Considerations in Animal Research

The research scientist should follow a rigid code of ethical treatment of experimental animals such as the one established by the National Society for Medical Research. This group includes representatives from such learned societies as the American Psychological Association, the American Medical Association, the Federation of American Societies for Experimental Biology, and the American Society for the Prevention of Cruelty to Animals (ASPCA). Here are the six rules established in 1979 by the American Psychological Association's Committee on Animal Research and Experimentation (2):

117

PRINCIPLES FOR THE CARE
AND USE OF ANIMALS

An investigator of animal behavior strives to advance our under-standing of basic behavioral principles and to contribute to the improvement of human health and welfare. In seeking these ends, the investigator should insure the welfare of the animals and should treat them humanely. Laws and regulations notwith-standing, the animal's immediate protection depends upon the scientist's own conscience. For this reason, the American Psy-chological Association has adopted the following Principles to guide individuals in their use of animals in research, teaching, and practical applications. All research conducted by members of the American Psychological Association or published in its journals must conform to these Principles.

1. The acquisition, care, use, and disposal of all animals shall be in compliance with current federal, state or provincial, and local laws and regulations.
2. A scientist trained in research methods and experienced in the care of laboratory animals shall closely supervise all pro-cedures involving animals and be responsible for insuring appropriate consideration of their comfort, health, and humane treatment.
3. Scientists shall insure that all individuals using animals under their supervision have received explicit instruction in experimental methods and in the care, maintenance, and handling of the species being used. Responsibilities and ac-tivities of individuals shall be consistent with their respective competencies.
4. Scientists shall make every effort to minimize discomfort, ill-ness, and pain to the animals. A procedure subjecting ani-mals to pain, stress, or privation shall be used only when an alternative procedure is unavailable and the goal is justified by its prospective scientific, educational, or applied value. Surgical procedures shall be performed under appropriate anesthesia; techniques to avoid infection and minimize pain must be followed during and after surgery. Euthanasia shall be prompt and humane.
5. Investigators are strongly urged to consult with the Commit-tee on Animal Research and Experimentation at any stage

preparatory to or during a research project for advice about the appropriateness of research procedures or ethical issues related to experiments involving animals. Concerned individuals with any questions concerning adherence to the Principles should consult with the Committee.

6. Apparent violations of these Principles shall be reported immediately to the facility supervisor whose signature appears below:

Name: _____

Position:_____ Phone:_____

If a satisfactory resolution is not achieved, a report should be made to the responsible institutional authority designated below:

Name: _____

Position:_____ Phone:_____

Unresolved allegations of serious or repeated violations should be referred to the APA Committee on Animal Research and Experimentation.

7. These Principles shall be conspicuously posted in every laboratory, teaching facility, and applied setting where animals are being used. All persons in each laboratory, classroom, or applied facility shall indicate by signature and date on the attached sheet that they have read these Principles.

Another important group concerned with improving the use and care of experimental animals is the Animal Welfare Institute (134), which has offered a policy on the use of vertebrate animals for experimentation and testing. They recommend that:

animals should be used for experimentation only (1) when there is no known feasible alternative; (2) after review of a carefully designed experiment based on knowledge of existing literature on the subject; (3) using the smallest possible number of animals; (4) of the most suitable species; (5) maintained in an optimum environment; (6) under the care of trained, sympathetic personnel; and (7) preventing pain, fear, and anxiety by judicious experimental design and generous use of anesthetic, analgesic, and tranquilizing drugs. (8) Endangered species should not be used. (9) Threatened species should only be used for experiments conforming with requirements for human experimentation.

The Information Report of the Animal Welfare Institute (134) lists a large number of painful experiments that have been conducted on animal subjects. In many of these experiments, careful experimental design could have lessened the number of animals used; in others where no clear hypotheses were delineated careful experimental design might have better ensured that some important scientific data could have been derived. What is particularly unfortunate is that a large number of these reported experiments were done by psychologists who did not entirely adhere to admonitions voiced by the American Psychological Association or by groups such as the Animal Welfare Institute. Experimental design is a crucial part of this. There is an old joke that has a person say, "I didn't have time to write a short report, so I'm writing a long one." On the surface that doesn't make much sense—but think about it. Does it not take more thought to pull together ideas in a succinct fashion than in a long-drawn-out, perhaps rambling manner? And might it not take more thought, care, and intelligence to design an experiment powerfully enough conceived so that one would not need a large number of animals to stumble upon the information?

A bill (H.R. 282) introduced into the House of Representatives in 1979 has as its major purpose "to promote the development of methods of research, experimentation and testing that minimize the use of, and pain and suffering to, live animals." The goal would be to support research into alternative methods —such as computer modeling and tissue culture techniques— that could provide in experiments answers currently dependent upon the use of live animals. Few people question the need, on occasion, to use animals for research, although there are extreme groups that would not allow any research using animals. The position of organizations concerned about animal welfare (such as the American Society for the Prevention of Cruelty to Animals and the Animal Welfare Institute) is that such experimentation may be necessary—there are many millions of diabetics alive today as a result of Frederick Banting's work on dogs—but that care and concern must be exercised.

A final note: In Principle 1 of the American Psychological Association Principles (p. 118), the scientist is held responsible for more than just the laboratory's handling and treatment of animals. As one can see, the *acquisition* of animals is another crucial concern. The possibility that family pets might be acquired by unscrupulous dealers and wind up in laboratories is not only an ethical concern for the research scientist but a legal one as well, for, as Principle 1 states, there are legal restrictions and requirements which apply to the treatment of animals. The interested student may find a detailed analysis of the legal rights of animals in a book by Emily Leavitt (92). Another view, by a researcher, is found in Maurice Visscher (142).

Ethical Considerations in Human Research

Over and above the problems of standard ethical research procedures with animals, special considerations arise when the subjects are humans. We strive for reality and control in experiments, and this is directly involved in the problem of ethical design and execution of research. Some years ago, a group of well-trained psychologists in the armed services were upbraided for doing research on stress under simulated combat conditions. One of their experiments went something like this: A recruit was taken into a "combat" area and left in a cave with the instructions that he was to remain in the cave while some blasting went on. He would be protected in the cave from any danger from the explosion. He was equipped with a radio which would receive but not transmit. Some time later there was an explosion. He was told over the radio that the explosion had sealed off the entrance to the cave but not to worry, that every effort was being taken to get him out. He was told at that time that if he wished to fix the radio so that it would transmit as well as receive he should follow instructions. He then received radioed instructions that went along the lines, "Take that blue wire leading from the snap lug marked 'C' and run it to the red terminal . . ." and so on, giving him explicit instructions which would make the radio capable of transmitting.

This was an excellent test of the ability to perform a fairly intricate task under stress. To tell him that he was in danger (a stress stimulus) and then to get him to perform a task such as wiring the radio was ingenious; the experimenter could objectively time the moment he radioed the stress stimulus and measure with precision the time elapsed between the radioed stress and the moment the subject came on the air with his own transmission. It was indeed ingenious and realistic as a stress study. It also had carefully controlled variables, making it an excellent representative design for an experiment. The experiment was, unfortunately, also highly questionable from the standpoint of ethics. The experimenters failed to take into consideration the need for consent by the subject to perform in such an experiment. While it demonstrates some good procedures, the risks involved to the health of the subject make it a doubtful one from the standpoint of an acceptable procedure. Inherent in this is the problem of irreversibility of damage. We do not know enough about the effects of stress on a human subject to say that such an experiment would not produce physiological changes that would be permanent and injurious—even without considering the risk of fatality, which might be a result of severe stress.

This technique of placing a person in a situation in which he believes he is in mortal danger is obviously more effective than asking him how he might behave under such circumstances, or asking him to act out such a situation. The simulation of stress is always a problem, as we saw in Chapter 7 in our discussion of isolation and confinement. Once again, Brunswik's representative design appears relevant. On pp. 94–5 we suggested this term to describe the optimal in experimental design: a minimum of artificiality and a maximum of control over the variables—that is, the problem studied should have reality and yet the variables should be carefully controlled. In this stress situation the question of representative design is important: Do you get realistic results at the risk of severe behavioral disruption or even losing a life (as in the case of the cave experiment), or do you sacrifice reality and use less disturbing techniques?

One answer lies in a paper by Irwin Berg in which he spells out the three basic elements of ethical research with human beings: *consent, confidentiality,* and *standard or acceptable procedure* (25). First, it is necessary always to get the *consent* of the subject in the experiment. "Where the information requested is highly personal or where the experiment involves some pain, discomfort, or risk, the subject should be made fully aware of what he is consenting to, at least in a general way." In the case of patients in psychiatric hospitals it is not always possible or meaningful—legally or morally—to gain the consent of mental patients, because they may be legally incapable of giving such consent. In such instances it is possible—with the consent of a patient's physician, family, or some other responsible person—to have a patient serve as a subject in a research project. With regard to the use of records (such as hospital records of cases), it is frequently not feasible to get the consent of the patient or the physician. The use of such records in research (or, perhaps, a textbook) is ethical "if the persons concerned are not harmed by the use of their records and their identities are not publicly revealed. . . ."

Informed Consent. Berg's suggestions about consent are important. In recent years the practice of obtaining informed consent from research subjects has been made a matter of ethical practice. Institutions receiving research support from the Public Health Service and the Department of Health, Education and Welfare have been obliged since 1966 to meet specific requirements of human-use committees. These committees review research proposals to make certain that subjects are protected and that the design and procedures proposed are ade-

quate. An important part of this review is the assurance that
the research subject has given informed consent, which means
that the subject knows in advance the purposes to be pursued
and the procedures to be followed in the course of the research,
and that he can freely withdraw at any time. Later in this chapter we will discuss the problem of experiments in which some
information must be withheld from the research subject or else
the whole purpose of the experiment would be vitiated.

I offer a personal example of an informed-consent form,
which appears as Appendix B (pp. 182-3). This is an actual
form used in research I am performing; it is not intended to
represent all such forms. Such forms differ widely from project
to project and from institution to institution, but the principles
remain the same—to inform the subject as precisely as possible
what is going to happen during the research. Appendix A (pp.
180-1)—also not universal—represents a review committee's
questions on such matters as potential risk to the subject as
well as steps taken to safeguard against such risks. These materials are presented to give you some idea of what an informed-
consent approach to research participation may involve. Also of
possible interest may be an article dealing with research involving
human subjects by Bradford Gray, Robert Cooke, and Arnold
Tannenbaum (72) and a comment by Allan Kimmel (85).

The problems of informed consent become more critical
when the research subject is a child. The same principles apply,
but it is evident that adults are in a better position to understand the purposes of research and the tasks involved. Certainly an adult would be in a position to consent to experimental procedures, whereas a child would not. The experimenter
should therefore gain the consent of the parents of the child, or
some responsible related adult, before beginning an experiment. Alfred Baldwin discusses these problems at some length
in a handbook on research with children (14). He points out the
necessity for explaining the purposes and plans of research to
the parents of children and answering with honesty any questions raised by them. Experimenters cannot allow themselves
the luxury of considering that the fears of parents are ground-

less, even though they know that nothing of potential harm may occur in the course of the research. An experimenter is also enjoined against unnecessary disruption of school or play time for the children in the conduct of the research. The convenience of the subjects should be a major consideration, rather than an experimenter's most convenient schedule.

Levy and Brackbill offer an interesting and seemingly effective means of obtaining informed consent more reliably in children (93). They observe that although the Department of Health, Education and Welfare has ruled that proxy consent (by parents or other adults) is not sufficient for research subjects over seven years of age, "no one really believes that seven-year-olds have the experiential background or intellectual sophistication to understand all facets of a complicated research project or the risks and benefits accruing to them or to children as a class." Levy and Brackbill initiated a project involving eight-year-old subjects who were brought to the university laboratory for a study involving the use of electrodes to measure ECG (electrocardiograms, heart patterns) and EEG (electroencephalograms, so-called "brain waves"). The electrical activity of the heart and brain were to be recorded and amplified so that a tracing of each could be obtained. The equipment and the electrodes, pasted to the chest and scalp areas respectively, could have seemed a threatening situation. The investigators used the following techniques to inform:

> Armed with a battery-operated videotape recorder equipped with a fast lens (for taping indoors without auxiliary lighting) and our eight-year-old pilot subject, we produced within approximately one hour a brief documentary program about the research. The tape followed the child from experimental start to finish: The child introduced himself and the experimenter to the unseen audience of peers; surveyed the terrain exterior to the laboratory facilities; walked into the laboratory where the equipment and procedures were described (the child was shown having the electrodes attached, serving in the study, having the electrodes

removed, etc.) and terminated with the child again directly addressing the camera for a salutory "See? That's all there is to it. Hope to see you again soon." Clearly the "story" was being told by one child to another. The experimenter's remarks were unnecessary. (93)

The technique worked so well with the children that they often hushed the experimenter if they were interrupted during the film viewing for any reason such as elaboration. Another finding was that some children corrected the experimenters if they deviated from the procedures shown on the videotape, such as not following the precise sequence of placing the electrodes on the scalp and chest areas. The technique has many benefits to recommend it in research with children.

Confidentiality. Let us turn now to the second of Berg's rubrics for ethical research planning, that of *confidentiality.* No subject would be happy about having others know of his or her performance on certain tasks nor of personal beliefs expressed on questionnaires. If a subject feels that the experimenter will not reveal confidential information, the subject can function more effectively in the role assigned. Psychologists are bound to the principle of confidentiality in their work. If they wish to use the results of a particular study and publish them, they must take care to ensure against the identification of any of their subjects.

The first two principles, consent and confidentiality, are illustrated in the well-known Kinsey report on sexual behavior. Kinsey used volunteers in his study of sexual practices. Every subject knew exactly the type of questions he would have to answer beforehand and had the opportunity to volunteer or withdraw. In addition, the reports were carefully prepared so that it was not possible for anyone who had participated in the study to be identified. Confidential handling of research data involving human subjects is critical for a relationship of trust between the public and the scientist.

The confidentiality of the material obtained in research with children is as critical as it is with adult subjects—perhaps even more so—because incalculable harm may be done to a child by a well-meaning experimenter who gives parents information about their children that they might not be able to comprehend or use objectively. This is particularly true when the research is conducted by inexperienced experimenters or when the materials used are psychological tests (which are used in research with children as well as adults). This use or misuse of the psychological test also happens in the clinical or school situation—a nonresearch area—and is described thus by L. J. Stone: "There seems to be general recognition of the great fluctuation and low predictive value of individual preschool tests. What is more, so general is the recognition of the doubtful predictive accuracy of an *individual* test, even for older children, that we are much less likely nowadays to find clinicians passing out IQs to parents to be worn like badges of honor or of shame. However, there are still a number of less cautious psychometricians and school testers (often not psychologists) who pass out this kind of unqualified datum far too freely and often produce in this way incalculable damage in the child's picture of himself or in his parents' appraisal of him" (137). This may also apply to results obtained in a nontest research situation.

Standard or Acceptable Procedure. The third of the basic principles governing the use of human subjects in research, as Berg outlines them, is that of *standard or acceptable procedure.* This assumes that the experimenter is trained and competent to use research procedures that his colleagues would accept as standard, that is, "tried many times before by many investigators." Now this poses a special problem, because research obviously cannot use the same procedures over and over again in all cases, if any originality is to occur. Original or novel procedures that are not standard must be regarded as acceptable by other competent investigators.

There are times when it may be necessary to hide the true purpose of the experiment from the subject. This is always a source of concern to the experimenter. For example, in a well-designed experiment reported by Ralph Hefferline *et al.* (78), the investigators wanted to see if they could condition a subject to make a muscle-twitch response so minute in strength that the subject would be unaware of making it. To record this minute twitch of the thumb, they hooked up an electrode and connected it to an electromyograph (which electrically records and amplifies muscle activity). The subjects in the experiment were listening to music, and noise was superimposed over the music. They could terminate the noise by the "unconscious" muscle twitch. The subjects were conditioned to this muscle twitch, of which they were unaware, and successfully stopped the unpleasant noise that interfered with their enjoyment of the music. When the subjects were told, in another phase of the experiment, to make a muscle twitch with their thumb to terminate the noise, they were unable to keep the response small enough.

If the subjects had been told originally of the purpose of the experiment, it would have been impossible to find out whether they could be conditioned to an unconscious avoidance response. Knowing the purpose would have made it conscious, and, as we have seen, they were unable to keep the response tiny enough when they consciously tried. This is a novel procedure; in a sense, the subjects were deceived by the experimenter in his instructions. They consented to an experiment without knowing the exact conditions. But this is not an unethical practice by any stretch of the imagination. The experimenters received a general consent to participate, did not violate the personal privacy of their subjects, subjected them to no discomfort, kept their confidence (although this type of experiment did not concern highly personal responses), and—most important in view of the original nature of the technique—kept to a procedure that would be highly acceptable to all competent psychologists.

These criteria in no way relieve the experimenter of the responsibility for being concerned about deception. No experimenter with human subjects feels completely comfortable in a deception experiment.

Some years ago a competent research psychologist, Evan Pattishall, and I decided to try an experiment to check out universal and personal validation. We were interested in seeing whether descriptive phrases to characterize personality could be so generally vague and universal as to be virtually meaningless. We were also interested in illustrating to students and professionals that meaningless universal terms are not very useful in working with people. We started with an experiment reported by Bertram Forer (65) in which he prepared a personality sketch largely derived from a newsstand book on astrology. Forer administered what he called his "Diagnostic Interest Blank" to an introductory psychology class and told the students that he would give each of them a personality sketch based on the test. The sketches were all identical, but the students did not know it. The sketches consisted of the following items:

1.   You have a great need for other people to like and admire you.
2.   You have a tendency to be critical of yourself.
3.   You have a great deal of unused capacity which you have not turned to your advantage.
4.   While you have some personality weaknesses, you are generally able to compensate for them.
5.   Your sexual adjustment has presented problems for you.
6.   Disciplined and self-controlled outside, you tend to be worrisome and insecure inside.
7.   At times you have serious doubts as to whether you have made the right decision or done the right thing.
8.   You prefer a certain amount of change and variety and become dissatisfied when hemmed in by restrictions and limitations.
9.   You pride yourself as an independent thinker and do not accept others' statements without satisfactory proof.
10. You have found it unwise to be too frank in revealing yourself to others.
11. At times you are extroverted, affable, sociable, while at other times you are introverted, wary, reserved.

12. Some of your aspirations tend to be pretty unrealistic.
13. Security is one of your major goals in life. (13)

Forer found that the "adequacy" of the test rated high; it was considered by the students to be a very good personality test. Pattishall and I decided to do a tighter analysis with a more statistical approach, using a standard anxiety scale for the sake of credibility. We administered the test to undergraduate and graduate students enrolled in courses in mental hygiene and advanced education psychology, as well as to psychiatric residents in training at the university hospital. The same general approach was taken—that we were going to administer a personality test, and then if the individuals wished we would give them a rating or personality description based upon it. As in the Forer experiment demonstration, the astrology book descriptions were given.

The results were similar to Forer's; most of the subjects felt that the items (except item 12) were true of themselves and (with the exception of item 6) were also true of other people. More students than psychiatric residents accepted the profile of being characteristic of themselves, but all subjects were about the same in attributing profile characteristics to other people. We believed that this was a good object lesson—that these universal statements illustrated descriptions that were so general as to be useless in analyzing individual subjects.

We did not count upon the ire engendered by the experiment. Indeed, some people said that they had been "duped," when it was explained to them that all the personality sketches were identical and that we were trying to demonstrate universal and personal validation. One psychiatric resident refused to speak to either one of the experimenters from then on, and in general a negative feeling occured in a number of the subjects. While this feeling diminished somewhat as the hoped-for educational implications of the experiment emerged, it nonetheless constituted a deception experiment with regrettable consequences in interpersonal contact.

As in the Hefferline experiment, not telling the purpose of

the experiment was essential to the design, but in both cases the subjects knew the purpose and results after the conclusion of the studies. (This important issue will be discussed further later.) I would like to concentrate for a moment on the design aspects of experiments in which deception is used. H. C. Kelman, in a discussion of deception in human experimentation (84), cites Martin Orne as observing that the use of deception "on the part of psychologists is so widely known in the college population that even if a psychologist is honest with the subjects, more often than not he will be distrusted." Think what a complex game this might occasion! The student is trying to figure out the "real" purpose of the experiment and act according to his or her own interpretation of what the experimenter wants, so, as Kelman notes, "the use of deception may actually produce an unspecifiable mixture of intended and unintended stimuli so that it becomes difficult to know exactly what the subject is responding to." A real part of the problem is the possibility that some stimuli might affect the experiment without intent. We know from operant conditioning research that smiles and frowns and nods and glancing at one's watch can alter the rate of verbal behavior. (Try looking frequently at your watch while talking to a friend and observe the reaction! [See p. 76.]) Is it not possible that such subtly and inadvertently presented stimuli might affect the subject? Take, for example, a study done a few years back by a group of social psychologists who were interested in the behavior of a cult that believed the end of the world was nigh. How would you act if you really believed that the world was coming to an end? (I know some friends who would open up a souvenir stand.) To study this behavior the psychologists joined the cult and professed to share the belief system, manifestly a deception technique. They felt that to come openly as psychologists to study the group would deny them full information, but to come as believers would allow them to get inside. To be sure, this was an interesting study with valuable data, but there is a nagging doubt about the ethics of dissembling to the cult and the possibility that unintended cues on the part of the experimenters—facial expressions, postural changes—might somehow have influenced the behavior of the persons studied. The world, by the way, did not end on the date predicted, and the study yielded valuable information about a group disrupted by a belief system that failed.

There are times when deliberate deception is not practiced, but the experimenters fail to explain the purpose of the experiment adequately to the subjects, perhaps because they do not think it important or assume that experimental subjects automatically behave as cooperative and relatively passive individuals. An experiment accomplished a few years ago with deep sea divers in a hyperbaric chamber illustrates the risks involved in not cooperating with the subjects. As part of a study to learn about physiological and biochemical change in humans under pressure, a deep sea dive was simulated, and urine specimens were obtained from each diver while in the chamber. No one really told the divers *why* the data were being gathered, assuming perhaps that they would automatically understand the relevance. How the divers themselves might have benefitted from the research was not explained adequately. It was learned later that the divers passed around the urine bottles and each urinated in all the bottles! (Even confidence-level statistics could not sort out *that* collection; a group urinalysis could not provide accurate *p* values.) The divers thought it was funny to fool around with the experiment. Had they been included as partners in the research a valuable opportunity for gathering important data might not have been wasted.

In sum, the treatment of the subjects in an experiment as *partners,* not as tools, requires consideration of these crucial steps:

1. The experimenter should carefully explain, as much as is possible and appropriate, the procedures and the purpose of the experiment. Why the data will be of help to the profession and what they will mean to the subject should be covered before the experiment.
2. During the experiment the subject should have a sense of partnership in working with the experimenter and should

be treated courteously and respectfully. (I know of one experimenter whose busy schedule often led to delay in or cancellation of experimental runs, inconveniencing the subjects enormously.) Subjects are not manila folders.

3. After the experiment, its procedures and its purpose often become imbedded in the results and their meaning. At this point, the experiment should be reviewed with the subjects. What occurred and what the experiment revealed is of considerable interest to most experimental subjects. Dismissing them summarily without fulfilling their curiosity (which, as you know, is the main motivator to researchers) is discourteous and also misses an opportunity to teach.

With respect to the third point, let me return to the experiment discussed earlier in which universal personality descriptions were given to subjects as their own personality profile. As noted, the debriefing engendered hostility in some subjects, but it was important to the purpose of instruction (as well as to ethical concern) that they be told the exact purpose and results as an object lesson.

Often subjects are not told and are left to wonder about the purpose—and indeed the results—of an experiment. What happens to a research subject *after* an experiment should be a source of concern for any experimenter. Debriefing the subject is not only courteous, but essential.

This is especially important in experiments with subjects who are going to become professionals. Most psychology students at one time or another are encouraged and expected to participate as subjects in experiments, to pick up experience that will be valuable in later life when they are conducting their own experiments. Too often they are used as subjects without any teaching context. Again, what happens to research subjects after an experiment is a matter of true concern for the experimenter. Research subjects should leave an experiment with a good feeling for what was done, why it was done, its importance, its relevance, what it meant to them as individuals.

Otherwise, the subject becomes a tool no more important than a relay on an electronic rack that might function for the purpose of the experiment.

This leads me to another important ethical consideration of the researcher—the use of research assistants. So far I have dealt with the research subject, but the assistant who helps in such stages as the preparation, conduct, and analysis of an experiment is often neglected. A research assistant often comes in on the middle of an experiment, and is programmed to run research—again, almost like a piece of equipment rather than an individual who wants to learn experimental technique. The proper research approach is to treat subjects and assistants as working partners. Then and only then can the experimenter maximize the value of the data and serve the important goal of using the research to teach as well.

One final word about acceptable and standard procedures: It is incumbent upon the psychologist conducting research to make absolutely sure that normal precautions are taken in all procedures. If using an electrical apparatus, it is vital to make certain all wires are properly insulated, that equipment is properly grounded, and so on. If the experiment requires physical exertion or stress, it is vital to have a physician's approval of the physical health of the subject. Normal caution and courtesy will preclude most of the possible problems that might arise in the use of human subjects in research.

With both adults and children, the ethical problems of research resolve themselves simply into the humane and considerate practices of interacting with other people. Catherine Landreth, in a letter to the *American Psychologist* published September 1961, invoked the image of Anna in *The King and I,* saying that understanding children and conducting research on them is "largely a matter of: getting to know them, getting to like them, when you are with them getting to know what to say, seeing it their way, as well as putting it your way, but nicely."

Let us end this discussion of ethics in human research by citing the principles adopted in 1977 by the American Psychological Association (61). (See pp. 118-9, where the principles regarding the use of animals are presented.) The publication by the APA in 1977 delineated nine principles of ethical standards for psychologists. Principle 9 is entitled "Pursuit of Research Activities" and is as follows:

PRINCIPLE 9.
Pursuit of Research Activities

The decision to undertake research should rest upon a considered judgment by the individual psychologist about how best to contribute to psychological science and to human welfare. Psychologists carry out their investigations with respect for the people who participate and with concern for their dignity and welfare.

a. In planning a study the investigator has the responsibility to make a careful evaluation of its ethical acceptability, taking into account the following additional principles for research with human beings. To the extent that this appraisal, weighing scientific and humane values, suggests a compromise of any principle, the investigator incurs an increasingly serious obligation to seek ethical advice and to observe stringent safeguards to protect the rights of the human research participants.

b. Responsibility for the establishment and maintenance of acceptable ethical practice in research always remains with the individual investigator. The investigator is also responsible for the ethical treatment of research participants by collaborators, assistants, students, and employees, all of whom, however, incur parallel obligations.

c. Ethical practice requires the investigator to inform the participant of all features of the research that might reasonably be expected to influence willingness to participate, and to explain all other aspects of the research about which the participant inquires. Failure to make full disclosure imposes additional force to the investigator's abiding responsibility to protect the welfare and dignity of the research participant.

d. Openness and honesty are essential characteristics of the relationship between investigator and research participant. When the methodological requirements of a study necessitate concealment or deception, the investigator is required to insure as soon as possible the participant's understanding of the

reasons for this action and of a sufficient justification for the
procedures employed.

e. Ethical practice requires the investigator to respect the individual's freedom to decline to participate in or withdraw
from research. The obligation to protect this freedom requires special vigilance when the investigator is in a position
of power over the participant, as, for example, when the participant is a student, client, employee, or otherwise is in a
dual relationship with the investigator.

f. Ethically acceptable research begins with the establishment of
a clear and fair agreement between the investigator and the
research participant that clarifies the responsibilities of each.
The investigator has the obligation to honor all promises and
commitments included in that agreement.

g. The ethical investigator protects participants from physical
and mental discomfort, harm, and danger. If a risk of such
consequences exists, the investigator is required to inform the
participant of that fact, secure consent before proceeding,
and take all possible measures to minimize distress. A research procedure must not be used if it is likely to cause serious or lasting harm to a participant.

h. After the data are collected, the investigator provides the participant with information about the nature of the study to
remove any misconceptions that may have arisen. Where scientific or human values justify delaying or withholding information, the investigator acquires a special responsibility to assure
that there are no damaging consequences for the participant.

i. When research procedures may result in undesirable consequences for the individual participant, the investigator has
the responsibility to detect and remove or correct these consequences, including, where relevant, long-term after-effects.

j. Information obtained about the individual research participants during the course of an investigation is confidential
unless otherwise agreed in advance. When the possibility exists that others may obtain access to such information, this
possibility, together with the plans for protecting confidentiality, must be explained to the participants as part of the procedure for obtaining informed consent.

k. A psychologist using animals in research adheres to the provi-
sions of the Rules Regarding Animals, drawn up by the Com-

mittee on Precautions and Standards in Animal Experimentation and adopted by the American Psychological Association.

l. Investigations of human participants using drugs should be conducted only in such settings as clinics, hospitals, or research facilities maintaining appropriate safeguards for the participants.

CHAPTER
10

The Scientist Communicating

*Give me a castle on the Rhine, a beautiful girl on an
operating table, a hunchback assistant, a roomful of
laboratory equipment, and I care not who makes this
nation's laws.*

—Hans Conreid

The scientist is sometimes pictured in pulp magazines and
cheap novels as a fiendish, inhuman, stooped, wild-haired
madman whose goal in life is to control the world. The very
term "mad scientist" conjures up images of such a figure in a
mountaintop laboratory with crackling lights and weird electrical gadgets and perhaps a few screaming people in large glass
bottles waiting for some terrifying experiment. Or perhaps at
the other end of the spectrum is the image of the absent-
minded scientist who forgets his umbrella, bumbling through
life dropping acid on his vest (alongside the gravy stains)—far
from fiendish but equally far from effective.

Both these pictures are arrant nonsense. But with regard to
psychologists in particular, recent years have brought a view of
them in some quarters as depth manipulators, manipulators of
the human mind. Vance Packard, in a book that came out a
number of years ago, *The Hidden Persuaders,* portrayed some
psychologists as invaders of the privacy of our very being. Recently in another book entitled *The People Shapers,* he pursues
the theme that some psychologists are trying to control every

facet of our daily behavior (104). He says there is an emerging "plastic" image of malleable man who can be controlled by programming behavior, by genetic manipulation, by test-tube babies, by computer files of persons.

In a world of diminishing privacy, with information of a private nature often residing in a credit bureau's computer, with psychological tests increasingly viewed as invasions of private space, with behavioral conditioning—and much therapy in general—perceived as some form of mind control, we need to concern ourselves with communication.

These are problems in what has been referred to as the public image of psychologists—what people think of them and their work. While far from strongly entrenched, such beliefs about the mad scientist or "depth-manipulator" qualities of psychologists do them injustice and are a disservice to science in general.

The Scientist's Communication to the Public

The necessity for operational definitions in science (Chapters 5 and 6) produces special problems in the communication of the scientist's work to nonscientific audiences. A common ground must be achieved between the technical language of science and the nontechnical language of everyday life. This conversion must be accomplished in such a way, however, as not to misrepresent the technical statement. This is a difficult task, and often as a result many journalists simply do not bother to insure a complete equivalence of meaning.

Speak to any scientist and you are likely to find a person who has been burned by popularization. Newspapers in our culture are not designed to be purveyors of scientific information; they are primarily a source of entertainment and news. Where scientific information generally appears (except in such papers as the *New York Times*) is in the magazine section of the Sunday paper, manifestly not a news section but rather an entertainment folio. Popular news sources often tend to give the reader a capsule education in science, as, for example, in a

deceptively simple account of relativity theory or medical research. So, alongside a story of Italian movie starlets, an article
about the problem of heroin usage among our troops in Ger-
many, recipes for Thanksgiving, and the favorite jokes of a TV
comic, will appear something about science, usually wrapped in
a mystique peculiar to such popularization, with standard words
such as "miracle," "wonder," and "marvel" underscoring the
inevitably "new" breakthrough of science. The researcher
whose preliminary work on a prosthetic device for amputees is
written up in a popular magazine under a title such as "Science
Brings New Hope to the Amputee"—in which an account of a
"miraculous" new artificial hand is splashed in color—is not
fairly or adequately represented.

A friend of mine had this very thing happen to him. A widely
circulated weekly magazine heard about his laboratory's work
on a new artificial hand and asked to write it up. His understanding was that it would be an account of a preliminary
nature on the experimental work that had gone into researching
and developing the prosthetic device. Instead, it was told as a
fait accompli, a miracle wrought in the laboratory. One tragic
consequence of such irresponsible handling of the story was a
deluge of phone calls to the laboratory and clinic where the
device was being developed. Irate and disillusioned veterans,
amputees who had been treated at the clinic, demanded to
know why this new miracle had been kept from them. It was a
hard job explaining that the device was still in the early stages
of research. It is this sort of experience that so often sours researchers on communication of information to the layman.

The perception of scientists by the layperson is often distorted in such a fashion, and yet it is impossible for scientists
not to be touched by the social impact of their research in some
fashion. As I have noted in another paper,

> The scientist has been considered something like a ser-
> vant god, offered homage but expected to produce
> miracles on command. And, as with all inefficient
> gods, the shamanistic scientist is often excoriated and

repudiated by his people, a fact which may make the scientist even less interested in leaving his laboratory and assuming his social responsibility. It is inevitable that a scientific discovery ultimately is expressed as social change and it is equally inevitable that the scientist must eventually perceive his work in a social context. (6)

In recent years, the support available for scientific research has increased markedly, particularly with the growth of funds appropriated by the federal government as well as private foundations. With this increased support there is a curious conviction held by many people that money is the answer to scientific searches. This may be related to what I have referred to above as the shamanistic quality of the scientist; as a magician he should be able to perform miracles, given enough money. The cure for cancer is one of the truly critical problems of our time, and the search for a solution to this disease requires money for apparatus, laboratories, and scientific personnel to carry on the research. But neither money nor the ability of dedicated scientists is *sufficient,* although each is *necessary.** For in addition to money and dedicated research in any one field, every science depends upon other scientists working in a variety of areas for new breakthroughs of information. For example, the electron microscope opened up new sources of information for neurology, and electronic computers made data processing possible as never before. With an advance in one science, then, progress *may* be made in others, although this is at best an uneven development. The search for a cure for cancer may come unexpectedly from a laboratory working on problems of virus disorders, or from other scientists whose efforts are not immediately directed toward this special research area. It is necessary to integrate many factors before a "breakthrough" is possible.

---

* Szent-Györgyi, with characteristic humor and pith, observed once, regarding the large amounts of money expended on supporting cancer research, that there were more people living off cancer than dying from it!

Selig Hecht discusses this with regard to the development of the atomic bomb:

> We should know that all the money in the world could not have built an atomic bomb in 1936. Atomic energy was known, and many of its properties were understood. It had been released in small quantities in laboratories, and its release in large quantities in the sun and the stars had been studied. But the critical information and the critical direction to follow for releasing it in large amounts on earth were lacking in 1936, and no one could have used two billion dollars for making an atomic bomb at that time. It is this that is important in understanding the relation of science to industry, to medicine, and to the public. There has to be knowledge before it can be applied. At a certain stage of scientific development, theoretically critical knowledge becomes available. Before that moment—which no one can guarantee in advance—the knowledge cannot be applied. After that moment application is reasonably certain and only the special technics for utilization need be worked out. (77)

I have described the negative side of communication with the laity only to explain why so many scientists are reluctant to present research information for popular consumption. There is, fortunately, another side to the story, found in the many highly responsible science writers, newspapers, and magazines. These individuals and media of communication represent what the French have called *haute vulgarisation* (literally, "high-level vulgarization"). They attempt to present scientific information in a manner comprehensible to the intelligent layman and as comprehensively as possible without doing injury to the information. Magazines such as *Scientific American* serve such a purpose extremely well. There are many excellent science writers who try to balance accuracy with interesting writing.

There is no doubt that the scientist has a responsibility for the communication of his research, first to his colleagues, next to the public. Ernest Renan, in 1848, wrote,

The specialist-*savant*, far from deserting the true arena of humanity, is the one who labours most efficaciously to the progress of the intellect, seeing that he alone can provide us with the materials for its constructions. But his researches cannot have an aim in themselves, for they do not contribute to make the author more perfect, they are of no value until they are introduced into the grand current.

This is echoed by Jean Rostand who in 1960 observed, "The ideal of the popularization of science (and here lies its moral value) is to develop and assist a community of thought."

The Scientist's Communication to Other Scientists

The necessity for communication among scientists is, perhaps, of even greater importance than is that of communicating scientific information to the public. Throughout this book, there have been references to the manner in which most scientific communication takes place through journals, books, papers presented at scientific meetings, and informal social contact. There are journals limited in large measure to the specific subject matter of the science, such as the *Journal of the Experimental Analysis of Behavior;* the *Journal of Comparative and Physiological Psychology;* the *American Psychologist* in the field of psychology; *Nuclear Physics;* the *Journal of the Optical Society of America;* and the *Journal of Biochemistry,* to name some examples from other scientific disciplines. Scientists tend to publish in their own discipline's journals or in journals that reach an audience of similar interests; for example, a psychologist working in the area of vision research might well publish in the *Journal of the Optical Society of America;* a biochemist engaged in research on brain chemistry might submit his or her writings to the journal *Experimental Neurology.* There are, in addition, several journals aimed at a broader scientific audience, such as the magazine *Scientific American,* in which scientists in varying disciplines can write for each other in a manner comprehensible also to the nonscientist. Another

weekly journal, *Science,* published by the American Association
for the Advancement of Science, reports research of a technical
nature and theoretical papers from all sciences in addition to
reports of political and public affairs of interest to the scientific
community. Now as never before there is an immense amount
of available literature in science. This in itself creates a significant problem for the scientist, who cannot easily keep up with
the spate of material pouring forth in journals. In recent years,
this phenomenon has been attacked as an exercise in data storage and retrieval through the use of computers. For the everyday reading of the average scientist a necessary compromise
must be made with the ideal of reading everything. He or she
selects perhaps a few journals to read with regularity, scans abstracts of published literature, and depends to some degree
upon colleagues to mention papers that might have been missed.

When an article appears in a professional scientific journal, it
usually follows a predetermined and generally accepted format.
Most articles will begin with an introduction and a review of the
literature, proceeding to a description of the experimental design,
a presentation of the results obtained in the experiment, a discussion of those results, and a summary, followed by a bibliography
of relevant articles. Such scientific papers are usually astringent
and formal, and in no way truly reflect the very informal, enjoyable aspects of sitting around in a laboratory with one's colleagues
and talking about the way research might be accomplished. The
end product is a dehydrated form of the entire story.

One of the problems that faces us in the United States is what
I refer to as a "conspiracy of efficiency." The American scientist
is much less relaxed than, for example, his British counterpart.
The journals make the research look exceptionally organized with
its inevitable progress from title to bibliography. This is an extremely well-organized and effective means of presenting the information,* but it is not necessarily the way research is organized.

---

* It is also likely that publication costs, which have soared over the
years, make a tighter presentation of the research data more effi-
cient—but infinitely much less fun.

The British are willing to allow an excursion into humor in the middle of the scientific discussion if it serves to elucidate or amuse. For example, in the middle of a discussion on rudimentary brain development British neurologist W. Grey Walter interrupts the flow of his essay to introduce a bit of doggerel. He talks about a dinosaur that had two brains: "One in his head, the usual place, the other at the spinal base. Thus, he could reason *a priori,* as well as *a posteriori*" (143).

The choice of an audience is in itself an interesting scientific function. If professional journals become the major avenue of scientific communication, then the reports will necessarily be brief because of constraints of space. Moreover, they will assume a common background of readership. For example, a psychologist reporting a psychoanalytic study would not be likely to define Freudian terms such as "id" or "superego" because he would assume that a person reading the journal would share a common knowledge of basic concept and theory. Similarly, an operant conditioner reporting research in the *Journal of the Experimental Analysis of Behavior* would not feel it necessary to define "schedules of reinforcement." There is, however, a need for some repository of this assumed background of shared knowledge, and this need, as T. Kuhn points out (88), is served by the scientific textbook.

The function of the textbook is "to expound the body of accepted theory, illustrate many or all of its successful applications, and compare these applications with exemplary observations and experiments" (89). The textbook, then, becomes for the scientific practitioner a statement of an agreed-upon body of theory and data, a model for his science. But it creates a problem in that the scientist—particularly the student scientist pressed for time—tends to rely increasingly on the text as a primary source of information and rarely goes back to original sources. Why need a student read Clark Hull or Edward Tolman in the original when current textbooks present the theoretical positions of these men in a lucid and systematic fashion? But the student interested in the *processes* underlying the developments in their theories must go to the research journals to recapture the flavor of the experimentation as the two schools advanced their somewhat competing positions. The textbook also presents a view of the development of a science that may appear oversimplified and selective. Science, as Thomas Kuhn observes, has little room for repudiated books, and "the result is a sometimes drastic distortion in the scientist's perception of his discipline's past. More than the practitioner of other creative fields, he comes to see [the past] as leading in a straight line to the discipline's present vantage" (90).

Not all texts are equivalent. If everything in a science were *fully* agreed upon, one textbook per field would suffice. Variations in textbooks (note the many introductory psychology textbooks) normally reflect differences in emphasis or style of presentation, although in fields where theoretical disagreements abound the textbooks may become a salvo in a battle for the advancement of one model over another.

It is true that the textbook itself often begins to assume some shared background of specialized knowledge. Most textbooks in science now are not addressed to the generally educated audience of interested layman (which includes scientists from other disciplines).

Contrast the average textbook of today with Darwin's *Origin of Species,* which was addressed to any literate person interested in the field, without special reference to practitioners. The need today is probably served as well as anywhere in the excellent journal *Scientific American,* addressed to the intelligent layman.

For practicing scientists the constraints of texts and journals are necessary for the advancement of their fields. But for the historian and philosopher of science, as well as for those who are generally interested in the creative process, the distillation of years of thought and experimentation into the formal research report (as I have observed a number of times in this book) is a loss.

Let me give you a personal example of such an event. In research that some of my associates and I were doing on verbal behavior in human subjects—recording and studying the verbal patterns of individuals and of these same individuals in group interaction—we were looking for some sort of reinforcer to use as a reward for speaking. Our subjects were paid by the hour for their participation. But it seemed to us, as we were sitting around talking about the experiment, that this was not an adequate reward for our purposes inasmuch as it did not matter how much or how loud the subject spoke during the session; the subject received the same amount no matter how much he or she talked. So we wondered what would happen if we tried to get the subject to speak louder or faster by rewarding such verbalization. Recognizing that money is a very good reward in our culture, we decided that it would be a fine idea to see what would happen if we paid the subject in money as he or she was speaking, so that each impulse spoken into the microphone would be rewarded. What would happen if we paid him or her by the spoken impulse? We thought that a coin dropping into a chute each time the subject spoke above a certain amplitude would be a good reinforcer to produce and maintain such behavior.

But then we started counting up the number of such impulses during an hour session, and found that there would be several hundred. It would be financially impossible to use coins unless we were to use pennies. In the course of this informal discussion, it was decided that pennies are not really very good rewards in our culture. A nickel seems to have more than five times the rewarding value of a penny. So the minimum successful financial reward in the form of a coin would probably be a nickel. However, if we used nickels, the experiment would become so rewarding that the experimenters would likely join the ranks of the subjects!

Someone suggested that we might try using poker chips that the subjects could exchange for money at the end of the session. In this way they would be working for a symbolic monetary reward that is very strongly reinforced in our culture. We talked about the meaning of poker chips and the images that poker chips conjure up in the minds of various people in a group. Stacks of poker chips in front of a gambler in a smoke-filled room and the various dramatic associations of poker chips in the folklore of our culture were discussed. Of course there was a lot of joking about this, and someone wanted to know if we would have to wear green eyeshades and roll up our sleeves and put garters on them, and whether we would have to use a round table with a green felt cloth over it, and so on, invoking the humor of the gambling situation. We finally decided to use chips.

The above account is merely a capsule record of the many hours of discussion on an informal level which went on during this particular part of the experiment. When the paper was finally written up for publication in professional journals, it merely reported, "Because of the generalized reinforcing nature of poker chips, they were used as a reinforcement for verbal behavior as a substitute for monetary reward (but symbolic of such secondary monetary reinforcement) and to be exchanged for money." Nothing about the green eyeshades, the green felt cloth, the sleeve-garters, the smoke-filled room—remarks which would be inappropriate for a scientific paper.

I do think that it is somewhat unfortunate that the joking and informality of group research discussions are filtered out by the time they appear in a published form. Students who might otherwise consider research as an enjoyable career are given the idea that research is a tedious, astringent, rigid discipline. In short, the careful always appears in print but rarely the casual. Where the casual does appear is in informal contacts among scientists, both in their own laboratories and in meetings such as conventions. If there is one important function served by a convention of scientists (who get together perhaps once a year), it is not the presentation of papers but the informal contacts in bars and restaurants which provide the opportunity for the exchange of ideas and information.

After Publication

What happens to research when it is published? It is probable, for one thing, that those individuals who have a special interest in the area covered by the research will evaluate the report in terms of their own experience, particularly if it departs from other findings in a significant manner. Readers will be likely to examine the data and the design of the research with a highly critical eye to see if any flaws in the research may gainsay the results. It is important—as we have seen in discussing operational approaches to research (Chapters 6–8)—for the experimenter to specify clearly what was done, so that another experimenter may replicate the experiment if desired.

As a body of literature grows in a particular area, the interest of researchers is stimulated and different aspects of the area come under more intensive study. As a body of information is developed and the evidence for or against a certain concept or theory piles up, researchers become convinced that one approach is better than another or that certain sets of facts indicate that condition A is in effect instead of conditions B and C. Although ideally this process occurs with complete impartiality, with the integrity and rationality so prized as the hallmarks of scientific research, nevertheless a human tendency to wish that one is right despite the evidence sometimes develops. When this occurs, the resulting resistance of scientists to the communication of others cannot help but affect the dissemination of information and its application. Earlier (pp. 18, 45) we have referred to the "pigheaded orthodoxy" of science to describe the tendency of scientists to resist new and different hypotheses, at the same time indicating that such a resistance is necessary in the interests of time, for qualified scientists cannot be expected to take time to disprove every theory, crackpot or not, that comes along. As I suggested before, it is up to the innovator to prove a point, while it is the responsibility of the community of science to listen. Thus the established scientific community must be as open-minded as the discoverer or innovator is reputable. The reputation of the experimenter is thus of prime importance in the evaluation of data.

Scientists Resisting

Given the integrity of the ideal scientist and granted the necessity for some resistance in the interests of time, why are there occasions when scientists resist data that challenge them? Barber, in an article on the history of scientific resistance to discovery, distinguishes several types of cultural resistance (15). One of these is that of *preconceived substantive conceptions and theories,* which often hinder discoveries. Even in the most industrious and talented of scientists this form of resistance can occur, as we have seen in "The Case of the Floppy-Eared Rabbits" discussed in Chapter 1. Remember hypothesis myopia?

Religious beliefs may also play a role. Whenever one thinks of conflicts between scientific and religious belief, it is usual to emphasize the position of the religious layman or theologian who resists ideas contrary to a religious system, but it is also possible for scientists who are deeply religious to resist theories or data that may challenge their own beliefs. A Victorian scientist, for example, who was devoutly religious might have been expected to resist a theory such as Darwin's, which might have challenged beliefs regarding the origins of man.

Barber lists still another source of possible resistance in the *social interaction of scientists.* As he observes,

> In general, higher professional standing in science is achieved by the more competent, those who have demonstrated their capacity for being creative in their own right and for judging the discoveries of others. But sometimes, when discoveries are made by scientists of lower standing, they are resisted by scientists of higher standing partly because of the authority the higher position provides. (16)

The monk Mendel was ignored for many years because of his lack of professional standing; the scientific societies then in existence were not interested in this nonscientist's quaint ideas about genetics.

For the most part, examples of resistance to scientific discovery occurred in the nineteenth century or earlier. Barber, for example, refers to the difficulties experienced by Faraday, Galton, Lavoisier, and Copernicus, among others, but these were scientists challenging established thought in a time of somewhat limited communication.

Resistance can and certainly does happen today, but I believe it is much less likely because of the very nature of science
as it has developed, from a rather limited and aristocratic pursuit—a gentleman's avocation, perhaps—to a truly democratic
system in which opportunities for status and success are mainly
contingent upon ability. Resistance is nevertheless a tendency
to guard against vigorously. Barber summarizes the problem:

> That some resistance occurs, that it has specifiable
> sources in culture and social interaction, that it may be
> in some measure inevitable, is not proof either that
> there is more resistance than acceptance in science or
> that scientists are no more open-minded than other
> men. On the contrary, the powerful norm of open-
> mindedness is science, the objective tests by which con-
> cepts and theories often can be validated, and the
> social mechanisms for ensuring competition among
> ideas new and old—all these make up a social system in
> which objectivity is greater than it is in other social
> areas, resistance less. The development of modern sci-
> ence demonstrates this ever so clearly. Nevertheless,
> some resistance remains, and it is this we seek to
> understand and thus perhaps to reduce. . . . As men in
> society, scientists are sometimes the agents, sometimes
> the objects, of resistance to their own discoveries. (17)

In summary, then, there must be a balance in scientific
communication to other scientists, just as there must be a balance in communication to the general public. The community
of scientists should be neither closed—resulting in oligarchy—
nor completely open—resulting in anarchy. As Bronowski has
stated,

> The society of scientists must be a democracy. It can
> keep alive and grow only by a constant tension between
> dissent and respect, between independence from the
> views of others and tolerance for them. The crux of the
> ethical problem is to fuse these, the private and the
> public needs. (35)

Science and Society

In its own society—which is a replica in miniature of the larger society, of which modern science is both the agent and the product—scientists are no more than citizens sharing a common culture; however, care should be taken that they are no less than scientists, following that special (and specialized) tradition indicated by Bronowski of independence, originality, and, as a product of these qualities, dissent (36).

It is absolutely imperative for scientists to communicate their knowledge as well as they can, accepting the social responsibility of education suggested by Renan, Rostand, and the Archbishop of York (who once told the British Association for the Advancement of Science that scientists "must educate their fellow countrymen to use rightly the inventions they have given them, and must make plain the terrifying results which may follow their wrong use").

It is easy enough to see the relevance of the archbishop's statement to nuclear physics and the threat of annihilation, but it is also relevant to psychology. In an address before the American Psychological Association in 1955, the brilliant physicist Robert Oppenheimer made the following observation about physics and psychology:

> In the last ten years the physicists have been extraordinarily noisy about the immense powers which, largely through their efforts, but through other efforts as well, have come into the possession of man, powers notably and strikingly for very large-scale and dreadful destruction. We have spoken of our responsibilities and of our obligations to society in terms that sound to me very provincial, because the psychologist can hardly do anything without realizing that for him the acquisition of knowledge opens up the most terrifying prospects of controlling what people do and how they think and how they behave and how they feel. This is true for all of you who are engaged in practice, and as the corpus of psychology gains in certitude and subtlety and skill, I can see that the physicist's pleas that what he dis-

covers be used with humanity and be used wisely will seem rather trivial compared to those pleas which you will have to make and for which you have to be responsible.

Science and the Social Order

In the preceding chapter the section dealing with ethical considerations was concerned, for the most part, with ethical procedures in the design and execution of research. Because the ethical concerns experienced by scientists in research are based on social responsibility, it may be of value to examine the ethics of scientists with respect to the social system in which they work and live. Science, as universal a realm as music, is affected as much as music by the culture in which it develops.

How does one evaluate a culture? One effective way is to examine those particular characteristics of a society that distinguish it from other societies. Kingsley Davis, for example, has delineated the characteristics of our own open-class society in a sociological analysis of the ethical system it has developed. This open-class ethic, he indicates, is as follows:

1. *Democratic* in the sense of favoring equal opportunity to rise socially by merit rather than by birth.
2. *Worldly* in emphasizing earthly values such as the pursuit of a calling, accumulation of wealth, and achievement of status.
3. But at the same time *ascetic* in stressing physical abstinence and stern sobriety, thrift, industry, and prudence.
4. *Individualistic* in placing responsibility on the individual himself for his economic, political, and religious destiny, and in stressing personal ambition, self-reliance, private enterprise, and entrepreneurial ability.
5. *Rationalistic* and *empirical* in assuming a world order discoverable through sensory observation of nature.
6. *Utilitarian* in pursuing practical ends with the best available means, and conceiving human welfare in secularized terms as attainable by human knowledge and action. (52)

Davis suggests that such an ethical system is functionally related to an open-class society such as ours. It is also obvious that the characteristics of such an ethical code are part and parcel of the science that has developed within our society; the emphasis on truth, industry, reason, and integrity so prized in our culture reach fruition in its scientific expression. Science as a system has adopted the ethics and values of the society, and has in turn contributed importantly towards the development and practice of these ethics and values. It is perhaps also true that science is somewhat ahead of the society in its emphasis on the individual. Integrity is not an abstraction in science, it is a crucial aspect of the everyday behavior of each scientist as a person. Bronowski has observed,

> Like the other creative activities which grew from the Renaissance, science has humanized our values. Men have asked for freedom, justice and respect precisely as the scientific spirit has spread among them. The dilemma of today is not that the human values cannot control a mechanical science. It is the other way about: the scientific spirit is more human than the machinery of governments. . . . Our conduct as states clings to a code of self-interest which science, like humanity, has long left behind. The body of technical science burdens and threatens us because we are trying to employ the body without the spirit, we are trying to buy the corpse of science. (37)

Hermann Bondi has discussed the human qualities of scientific endeavors (26). Emphasizing in particular the need for testing to counter human fallibility, he suggests that science, more than any other enterprise, reckons with human error. "Because anybody may be wrong, it is pointless to refer to authority, for great scientists can be no less wrong than others. . . . It is through this insistence on checking that science has become universal" (27). Theories must be worked out so that they may be testable, so that people may work together to build knowledge. It is especially this quality of working together that makes for the humanized science of which Bronowski and Bondi speak. Bondi goes on to observe,

> Not long ago a history don wrote in an educational journal that he felt that, since present problems were largely problems of human relations, an education in the humanities, which dealt with human beings, fitted people better for this world than an education in science, which dealt with facts. This statement is nonsense. Science is a human endeavor and, moreover, it is the human endeavor in which world wide co-operation has been more successful than in any other. It is a human endeavor singularly well tailored to human abilities and human failings. If anything can teach you to co-operate with other human beings, irrespective of race or religion, ideology or nationality, then it is science. In this sense it is perhaps a far more human subject than the so-called humanities, and to speak about it as dealing impersonally, solitarily, with facts is so gross a misunderstanding of what science is, that it comes as a shock to realize that such views can still be held. (28)

To say, as Bondi does, that science is sometimes misunderstood is not to plead for some vague, uncritical acceptance by the nonscientist, but rather to indicate the responsibility of the nonscientist to make a genuine attempt to comprehend. The history don to whom Bondi refers renders, as a layman outside of science, uncritical judgment, for it is his responsibility to understand science and scientists, just as it is, as we have seen, the scientist's responsibility to make himself understood.

One of the purposes of this little book, besides that of introducing some information about scientific methodology, is to acquaint the nonscientist with some characteristics of the scientist and the scientific life. It can be no more than an introduction to the rigor, the flexibility, the fun and frustration, the mechanics, and the humanity of research.

CHAPTER
11

Communicating Research: How to Read and Write a Research Report

The way to write is well, and how you do it is your own business.

—A. J. Liebling

You may believe that your chances of writing a research report are remote at the present stage of your development as a psychologist. This may well be true, but there are other aspects of writing that will always be important to you. One aspect is learning how to *read* a research report, which you will surely have to do as a student; another is realizing that writing a research report is not significantly different from writing general term papers or scientific papers and that certainly you will be engaged in one or both of these activities.

To say that reading a research report is the obverse of writing one is a simple statement; if you can read and understand a report of an experiment then you should know the principles of writing one. In Chapter 6 we saw that the operational definitions of an experiment and the variables to be studied constituted, in effect, a recipe of how to do the research in a manner that will allow other, experienced researchers to evaluate it and, if desired, replicate the work. If the report is unclear or nonspecific in terms of materials and methods used, or vague as to the character of the subject population, it cannot be read intel-

156

ligibly, and therefore the work is not replicable. Moreover, its potential contribution to scientific knowledge cannot be assessed.

Clarity in Communication

This brief introduction to writing a report will concentrate on one major aspect of preparing an intelligent and intelligible report—the aspect of *clarity*. Clarity is the goal of good writers. Assuming you have some knowledge in a given area, you should not always assume the entire blame if you are unable to comprehend an article or paper in that area. Only if it is well written and has clarity has the author's responsibility to communicate been fulfilled. Science, as we have seen, is not a private matter—it must be public, open to evaluation, capable of advancing knowledge. Incomprehensibility does not equal brilliance; unfortunately, as Steve Aaronson has noted, scientists often believe that they had better "*sound* scientific" (I), which often means using jargon instead of clear language. A good example of writing that tries to "sound scientific" came to my attention recently as I reviewed an article cited in *Psychological Abstracts*. The abstract spoke of apprehension related to the "active encoding of written messages." I think the authors here were talking about "writer's block." There are times when scientific definitions are infinitely better than daily language (again, see Chapter 6), but the use of words in scientific definitions is not equivalent to the use of unclear language. To substitute "twenty four hours' food deprivation" for "hungry," as we have seen, is to make a concept operationally more sound without losing clarity.

The jargon about which we have concern is that which obscures. The social sciences seem most vulnerable to jargon. As you will recall, we have discussed the problem of developing a clear data language in psychology. Sociology is rife with jargon, examples of which are offered by Aaronson: "Consider such phrases as *coherent social consciousness, situational interactors,* and *adjustment alternatives*" *(1, p. 9).* Why is this so? In part, it is because writers in some scientific endeavors probably believe their writing should sound "scientific" and somehow arcane and mysterious to the layman. It may be, as Robert Day observes (54), quoting a humorous cynic: "A scientific paper is not designed to be read. It is designed to be published."

True science is public and *must* be readily communicated. The rule is: Don't use jargon that obscures meaning; use terms that have operational validity and clarity of communication.

One of my favorite examples, with which I will leave the topic of jargon, is drawn from Orwell (102), who, in an essay entitled "Politics and the English Language," rewrote this famous passage from Ecclesiastes:

> I returned, and saw under the sun, that the race is not to the swift, nor the battle to the strong, neither yet bread to the wise, nor yet riches to men of understanding, nor yet favour to men of skill; but time and chance happeneth to them all.

Orwell rewrote this to fit into modern jargon:

> Objective consideration of contemporary phenomena compels the conclusion that success or failure in competitive activities exhibits no tendency to be commensurate with innate capacity, but that a considerable element of the unpredictable must invariably be taken into account. (102, p. 84)

As an exercise, for your own amusement, take a clear passage such as the Biblical quotation from Ecclesiastes and rewrite it in jargonese.

Clarity in Writing

In the same essay Orwell offers six rules for clear writing. I should like to quote these rules, along with my added comments.

> *1. Never use a metaphor, simile or other figure of speech which you are used to seeing in print.*

This rule refers, largely, to clichés and phrases that are hackneyed. There is nothing intrinsically wrong with saying that something is "as sound as a dollar" (unfolding events may at times make this questionable), nor in scientific writing to refer to discoveries as "momentous." It is just not clear, imaginative writing.

2. Never use a long word where a short one will do.

Do not use "utilize" when "use" will do. There are exceptions to this rule—especially when you wish to vary style for more interesting writing—but in general "many" is just as good as "numerous."

3. If it is possible to cut a word out, always cut it out.

Brevity has many advantages. If you can make a passage brief without injuring clarity, by all means do so.

4. Never use the passive where you can use the active.

This is the keystone of Orwell's rules. Good writing is almost always active rather than passive. Instead of saying, "These principles were demonstrated by numerous experiments," try, "A series of experiments demonstrated that. . . ."

5. Never use a foreign phrase, a scientific word or a jargon word if you can think of an everyday English equivalent.

This rule is offered with the oft-repeated reminder that the substituted word must have operational validity.

6. Break any of these rules sooner than say anything outright barbarous.

This admonition is not a license to write badly. Orwell means that there are times when you cannot rigidly follow rules and still maintain good writing. For example, good style—which underpins good writing—demands that some variety is needed to maintain interest. The cadence of a passage—its rhythm—supports style; short, active sentences should prevail, but the rhythm of a paragraph is enhanced by varying sentence length. Rigid grammar is another problem, illustrated best by the jocular comment made by Winston Churchill when asked what he thought of ending a sentence with a preposition: "This is the sort of English up with which I will not put!"

Clarity Through Good Grammar

Good grammar is a means by which clarity can be achieved. Let us consider an example of a sentence that sounds reasonable but is grammatically weak, thereby creating ambiguity:

> The experimenter's dog was fed, so he left the laboratory.

Who left the laboratory, the experimenter or the dog? The grammatically correct way of expressing this event is a bit more convoluted, but clear:

> The experimenter, having fed the dog, left the laboratory.

A choice example of a dangling particle involving another dog is offered by Lois Fagin:

> After closing the incision, the dog was placed in a restraining cage.

Here, Fagin notes, " 'dog' is the subject of 'closing.' Any dog talented enough to close an incision certainly doesn't deserve to be put in a restraining cage" (62).

Enough of that type of example. The message is simple: Grammar is important in writing—as is punctuation—to make communication clear. The second underlying message is that you should already be a reasonably clear communicator—by dint of the years of training you have had. You were probably handling clear communication long before you could discriminate a present perfect tense from a past perfect tense. (Can you do this now?) My favorite illustration of this state of affairs comes from Molière's play from the late seventeenth century, *Le Bourgeois Gentilhomme* ("The Bourgeois Gentleman"). The play is a saga of a man of common birth who inherits wealth late in life and takes advantage of experiences long denied him. At one point he discovers, much to his delight, that he has been speaking *prose* all of his life!

Trust your ears—if a sentence doesn't sound right when you read it aloud, then it is probably an unacceptable sentence. The speaking style and writing style of a person are closely correlated. Not all spoken passages are clear and comprehensible, but we all know inarticulate people who cannot speak fluently but who are effective communicators. Their communication may be on a level limited to ordering from a menu, asking directions around a strange town, or issuing pithy comments about a certain professor, but these persons are nonetheless communicating and expressing ideas. From that base, the development of more effective speaking and writing for, let us say, classroom presentation or publication may begin.

Style

Each individual has his or her own style of writing and speaking. For example, each of us learned handwriting as a child in a relatively fixed, standardized fashion, painstakingly copying models of letters. Such standardization is not reflected in the handwriting each of us shows now, although there is a common universal structure. Many factors of experience and learning effect changes from the original learning experiences, yet there is a distinctive quality that marks the individual. You have no problem in identifying the individual whose letter you hold in your hand from the handwriting on the envelope, nor do you have trouble identifying a familiar individual by voice. Both instances illustrate how personal style can characterize an individual. This style should be polished for writing, polished by learning rules of communication that will enhance an individual's style and not injure it. In other words, good grammar or writing rules should not—and need not—submerge your personal style in writing.

Each individual's style is the basis of communicating by speech or writing. As we have noted, personal style is superimposed upon standardized speech and writing so that we learn individual identity by a host of subtle and obvious cues with which we are able to single out an individual.

An example of differences in style may be drawn from these samples taken from Faulkner and Hemingway.

> So we took the lunch box Miss Ballenbaugh had packed for us and the block and tackle and axe and shovel and our shoes and stockings and my pants (we couldn't do anything about the automobile, besides being a waster of work until we could reach Memphis, where surely— at least we hoped—there wouldn't be any more mud-holes) and went back down to the creek and washed the tools off and coiled down the block and tackle. And there wasn't much to be done about Boon's and Ned's clothes either, though Boon got bodily into the water, clothes and all, and washed himself off and tried to persuade Ned to follow suit since he—Boon— had a change of clothes in his grip.
>
> [William Faulkner, *The Reivers*]

> Miss Gage looked. They had me look in a glass. The whites of the eyes were yellow and it was the jaundice. I was sick for two weeks with it. For that reason we did not spend a convalescent leave together. We had planned to go to Pallanza on Lake Maggiore. It is nice there in the fall when the leaves turn.
>
> [Ernest Hemingway, *Farewell to Arms*]

The characteristic style of each author comes through clearly in these passages.

You should analyze your own speaking style as well as your writing style. Do you have, for example, vocal or written mannerisms that may interfere with full or fluent communication? Among the more frequent spoken mannerisms—not necessarily interfering but not contributing to good verbalization—is the use of "you know?" salted throughout conversation. This is one mannerism by which artificial attention is engendered: "You know what happened this morning?" The natural response, of course, is, "No, what happened?" Such dialogue is perfectly common, but not terribly exciting.

In writing you should also be aware of mannerisms. We meet the creation of artificial attention in phrases such as, "It is interesting to note that. . . ." If it is interesting, note it. Look at a piece of your own writing from a recent period. What is the average sentence length? Do you have repetitive phrases that appear overly frequently? How do you use punctuation? Read a passage aloud. Does it sound clear? Can you identify clauses in the vocalization of your writing? These are some of the ways you can assess your own work.

Of course, there are highly sophisticated methods by which such analyses can be done. One of these is to apply statistical methods not only to sentence length but also to potential differences between spoken and written utterances. In recent years techniques made possible by computer analysis have advanced the knowledge of linguistics and style. One such technique is reported in a 1969 work by a colleague and me in which a computer analysis of speech revealed information about personal style (59). We took vocal samples of various public figures, including President John F. Kennedy, and ran them through an analysis. You may recall what JFK's speeches sounded like. Theodore Sorensen has described the specific criteria Kennedy's speechwriters met in order to best get ideas across to audiences (132). These included short speeches, short clauses, and short words. Take this example from a Kennedy speech— his inaugural address, 20 January 1961:

All this will not be finished in the first one hundred days, nor will it be finished in the first one thousand days, nor in the life of this administration, nor even perhaps in our lifetime on this planet. But let us begin.

What John Dreher and I did was to take samples such as this and do a vocal rhythm analysis—i.e., measure objectively the repetitive pattern of talking and being silent, giving the duration of speech and silence that characterize the rhythm. This sample was then further analyzed into a continuous pattern; that is, the vocal rhythm analysis. We also compared the inaugural address with the speech President Kennedy gave during the Cuban missile crisis in 1962. (See figure.)

PERIODIC COMPONENTS OF DELIVERY
KENNEDY

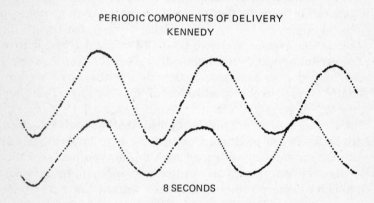

8 SECONDS

Top trace is Inaugural Address; bottom trace represents Cuban Crisis speech.

The two samples—portions of the entire speeches—show a remarkable similarity, made even more remarkable because one would assume that the Cuban crisis speech would have more emotional communication than the inaugural address, or would at least be of a different nature. The similarity in the two samples suggests that Kennedy's style of speaking was indeed one of short utterances and pauses. Moreover, the kinesics associated with his speaking—the gestures he used—fit the pattern. As Sorensen tells us, Kennedy used short jabs with his hands to emphasize certain points. And a study of his written words shows an equally deliberate stylistic structuring for effect. We can assume that in large measure, as Sorensen suggests, JFK's style was conscious and created for an audience effect.

What has this sophistication of stylistic analysis to contribute to your own writing and speaking? At the very least, it may make you aware of your vocal and written production as you engage in these important communication activities. Kennedy was highly aware of the need to communicate. His style would have delighted the political critic Orwell immensely.

English as a Pride and a Problem

You have decided advantages and disadvantages in being a speaker of English. For one thing, English is possibly the richest language for varied and colorful communication. In Chapter 6 we commented on the variety of words available for describing flocking behavior: *prides* of lion, *herds* of cattle, and so on— somewhat puzzling as to function, but certainly rich. The actor and linguist Tony Randall has commented on the richness of English, and points out that in English we can differentiate between "sky" and "heaven" while our friends who speak Spanish, Italian, or French need to use the same word for both. Such differentiation may not always be important, but it is true that English has variety. It is also true that English is powerful in that you can do terrible things to an English passage and, somehow, emerge with the meaning relatively intact. Bill Bryson, in an article entitled "Fractured English," offers a number of such examples of massacre and emergence (39), including these instructions in a hotel elevator in Belgrade: "To move the cabin, push button for wishing floor. If the cabin should enter more persons, each one should press number of wishing floor. Driving is then going by natural order." Or this gem from a hotel in Yugoslavia: "The flattening of underwear with pleasure is the job of the chambermaid. Turn to her straightaway." Or this example from a Tokyo hotel: "Is forbidden to steal the hotel towels please. If you are not person to do such thing is please not to read notis."

The richness of English also creates problems. There is more room for ambiguity. And there is also confusion in, for example, the fact that one can either "slow up" or "slow down"—both being equal. And, as Bryson notes, "The simple word 'set' has 58 uses as a noun, 126 as a verb, and 10 as a participial adjective" (39).

Recently, a choice example of ambiguity appeared in a government request for information from small businessmen. One of the questions on the form was, "How many employees do you have, broken down by sex?" One reply came back: "None, our big problem is alcohol."

English is so rich that you can convey myriads of meanings, but the very nature of this variety of words and meanings makes it imperative that you temper communication with clarity.

Writing a Report

I have dwelt, perhaps overlong, on the aspects of style that underlie communication, for it is style indeed that enables expression to float (or sink). Now let us begin to consider the means by which you can couple your writing ability with your research talents to produce a report.

Research is basic to many of our daily activities, even though we may not consider it as such. Finding the best dry cleaner or the finest Korean restaurant in town becomes a research effort as you gather information, make comparisons, and analyze performance based on defined criteria of excellence. Research always begins with an identification of the sources of information relevant to the topic. If you were going to put together a term paper on the topic of *learning*, let us say, you would be likely first to seek out the *Psychological Abstracts,* published by the American Psychological Association. There you would learn, to your astonishment perhaps, that between the years 1967 and 1977 there appeared 21,678 abstracts on the topic of learning. Obviously, the topic of learning is too broad, so you would have to refine your topic further, narrowing the area of interest to a subject that is more specific and manipulable.

1. *The investigative report.* This is a report of a piece of original research conducted by the experimenter or clinician.

2. *The interpretive report.* This may be a comment on work done by others or, more likely, a review. A review is a synthesis of the work of other investigators, assembled to present a coherent and cohesive overview of a specific area. It may be further subdivided into (a) *a narrative review,* an assembly of reports of research without author comment, and (b) *a critical review,* which is more than a reporting of the work of others because it includes the reviewer's evaluations as to the acceptability of the experimental design or other salient points relevant to the research reported. In other words, the narrative review offers an overview of the important work in the selected area, and the critical review assesses the research reports as to the value of the work. The critical reviewer may say, for example, that work reported by certain authors cannot be accepted because of flaws in their experimental design. Perhaps the animal selected for the research was not an appropriate subject or the statistics were not handled properly. This, clearly, would be a *judgmental* review, and the reviewer who criticizes must be on firm ground. Narrative reviews, although much safer for the reviewer, may not be as valuable to the field in the long run. The critical review obviously must be done at a level of research development that is mature.

Until further experience is available to you as a student, it is probable that the type of research report in which you will be active is the narrative review, which, as an assigned topic or a term paper selected by yourself, will require identifying sources of information, selecting a reasonable topic area, and then proceeding to gather information. The information-gathering stage, the "leg-work," will probably consist of library work to draw information from published sources, but it need not be so. For example, suppose you have decided to review the facilities in your community that provide services to old people.

Then your information sources would not be a published collection but a list of agencies serving the aged. Your leg-work would literally be to visit the various agencies to learn what is provided by way of legal aid, recreation, medical care, and similar services. In essence, you would be developing a type of case report such as we discussed in Chapter 2.

Whether your legwork is in the library searching through books and scientific journals or strolling from one clinic to another, your information gathering must be carefully done. Take notes. Index cards of the 3" x 5" size are handy, and will allow you to sort out the material later. In library work, it is essential that you keep continuous account of references. Many an author has found to his dismay that he had jotted "Freud, p. 12" on the back of an envelope salvaged from a telephone bill, only to wonder, when the final assembly of references was to be done, where in Freud's name that particular citation came from. It is best to record immediately the full name of the cited author (or authors) on an index card, then the complete title of the article (or book) and the journal, year, volume, and pages covered by the article. Use of this method of recording also makes it easier to alphabetize the references later, rather than having to sort through a list of citations on a sheet of paper.

What have we so far? The stages in researching and reporting are

1. identifying information sources,
2. selecting a workable problem or topic, and
3. gathering the relevant information.

Now we approach a fourth stage, in which you will sort through the information you have garnered, sift out the best relevant material, and organize the information to form a cohesive whole. To accomplish this, you will find it advisable to develop an outline immediately. Your outline should be the one with which you feel most comfortable in sorting out the data, but it is likely that you will be able best to develop an effective outline if you follow the anatomical structure of a research report. From the head (the title of the paper) to the feet (the references), the anatomical sketch of a paper provides a logical unfolding of information.

Guide to the Anatomy of a Report

In the following sections we are going to take up the individual parts of a report and discuss them. Some elements are common to both reviews and experimental investigations. The following diagram is intended to illustrate which elements are distinct to each type of report and which are common.

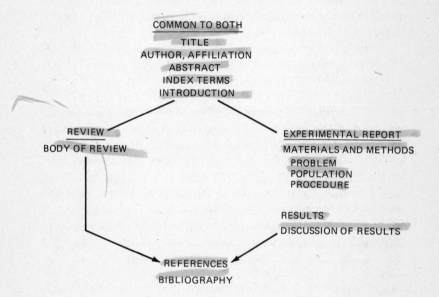

The Title.   As you use information to seek out data about your topic, you will learn that titles are the very basis of information retrieval. A good title leads to the material. For this reason, when you think of a title for your report, think of it in terms of someone looking it up in the literature as you have done. Information specialists who are dedicated to effective information storage and retrieval suggest that the title be "computer compatible"—i.e., consistent with the means of locating information related to the search. Titles should summarize the thrust of the report; they should be able to stand by themselves as concise summaries of what is reported. They should not be "cute" or insufficiently clear or misleading. Sometimes, being misleading is not entirely the fault of the author. In one search, I found a paper that had a title along the lines of "Concrete Stress Behavior Underwater," which sounded ideal to me inasmuch as I was conducting research with human divers under pressure and was interested in stress response. When I had the article in front of me it turned out to be an engineering analysis of stress on concrete pilings (such as those that support bridges) underwater. Of course, I was at fault as well as the author. The title was tempting. Had I checked the name of the journal carefully I would have realized that its reports were probably more concrete than I had imagined!

The Abstract. The abstract is probably the most important part of the paper. It is the part of the report that is read after the title. The individual searching for information is, as we have seen, led to the paper by the title. The abstract then serves the purpose of telling the searcher whether or not the particular report is of interest. In this regard it is sometimes the *only* part of the report to be read, and should therefore be well done. The abstract is, along with the title, the only part of a paper that will be stored for information retrieval, and, along with the title, is the means by which researchers find relevant material. The publication of abstracts is now the major retrieval aspect of a scientific publication. Many publications consist solely of abstracts: for instance, *Index Medicus* and others such as *Psychological Abstracts, Chemical Abstracts,* and *Biological Abstracts* which are published by scientific societies and contain brief abstracts of published scientific work, drawn mostly from journals. Books of abstracts such as *Underwater Medicine and Related Sciences* (114) are published regularly. Most scientific meetings—such as the annual convention of the Federation of American Societies for Experimental

Biology—publish abstracts of papers that will be presented (or, if published after the meeting, have already been presented); these become sources of information retrieval as well as programs for individuals who attend the meetings. Indeed, the most frequent means by which scientific papers are selected for inclusion at a meeting is by individuals submitting abstracts of their research to be considered. Thus, the abstract has become the central communication element in scientific work.

The abstract may be of two types, the *indicative* (or *descriptive*) abstracts, which is limited to a brief statement of the study reported without detail, and the *informative* abstract—the usual type of abstract encountered in scientific meetings and publications—which is, in effect, a condensation of the paper or report. The informative abstract stands alone. It is independent, as well it should if it is to be the only part of the report that is read. It should inform the reader of the general purpose of the paper; provide a statement of the problem studied, along with the methods used to study it; report the main results obtained in the study; and, finally, state what conclusions might be drawn from the experiments (or review) and the general significance for the field.

Returning to the abstract as a scientific communication submitted for presentation at a meeting, it is becoming increasingly true that indicative abstracts are losing favor and informative abstracts are being required. This detailed type of abstract is at times referred to as a "minipaper" or "synoptic."

A final note: The abstract that appears at the beginning of a paper has virtually ruled out the use of summaries, which were at one time popular. A summary is *not* an abstract; if it is used in a report, it should be brief, giving only the general conclusions of the study.

Index Terms.   Index terms—also known as *key words*—are required when a manuscript is submitted to a journal for possible publication. Index terms are words that are computer compatible and can lead the researcher through the body of literature to the report in which he has an interest. Usually at least three terms are required, being words *other* than those in the title. They should show whether the research subjects were human or animal; if the animals were studied, the species should be indicated. As an example, for my article entitled "Psychophysiological Factors in Diving" (10), prepared for physicians who treat divers, I might have chosen among these words: stress, panic, accidents, hyperventilation, cardiovascular changes, diver.

The Introduction. Often the introduction to a report is not labeled as such: It appears as a set of paragraphs that lead the reader into the body proper of the report. Whether or not it is labeled, the introduction should be a brief statement of the general area in which the research falls and a review of the important and relevant research that has been accomplished in the past, which leads in turn to a statement of the experiment to be reported, why it was conceived, and what relationship (along with the proposed research strategy) it has to past research. Reviews of past work once were more extensive than normally is found in current literature. Historical, scholarly reviews, containing statements of relevance to the current study, served as introductions to papers. Largely as a function of printing costs, I believe, the historical review that once served as an introduction has now yielded to the briefer statement. Nonetheless, the introduction remains a rationale and a bridge with existing knowledge, and provides continuity to a field of research.

An introduction to a review is different from an introduction to an experimental report in that it is more concerned with the reasons the review was attempted and obviously does not need to relate to new experimentation to be reported.

Materials and Methods. In the investigative report the section usually referred to as "materials and methods" is the basis of the experimental design as the reader will receive it. In clinical investigative studies—such as case reports as well as experimental reports—it is imperative that there be a clear explanation of the exact procedures used in conducting the research.

The report will usually be clearer if the writer departs somewhat from the usual materials and methods to break down this section into three more specific elements: stating the *problem* and specifying the *population* and *procedure.*

The background provided by the introduction has set the stage for the specification of the particular *problem* or *hypothesis* (see Chapter 5).

The hypothesis to be tested should be clear, specific, and testable. By testable I mean that any changes measured at the end of the study should be a result of the experimental manipulations by the investigator, not a product of chance factors. Stating an hypothesis clearly allows for determining the experimental effect.

The *population* section must specify the subjects used in the experiment or case study. In the case of human subjects, it is important to state clearly what the subject population consists of in terms of sex, age, and related factors. For example, do not say "middle aged"; say "forty to fifty-five years of age," if that is the age range. The basis of the selection is also crucial: How were the subjects chosen for this experiment or study? What is the number of subjects? From where were they drawn?

In animal research, it is equally important to specify number of subjects, sex, and age, in addition to genus, species, and strain (e.g., *Rattus norvegicus,* Sprague-Dawley descended). Species and, indeed, strain differences can be crucial. If these are unclear, another investigator, evaluating the experiment, could readily interpret results in mistaken terms rather than in terms of the hypothesis stated at the beginning of the report.

Because we continually set for ourselves the requirement that a research report should *(a)* allow a reader to evaluate the experiment or study as to the soundness of the approach, and *(b)* allow another investigator to replicate the study if desired, the *procedures* used must be clear and in sufficient detail to accomplish these goals.

In the discussion of the population section above, we saw the need for detailed specificity. In considering procedural requirements, you should go further and discuss how experimental and control groups were determined. In human experiments and case studies, it is important that you detail any instructions given to the subject, another factor that might alter results. Simple word-cues might have effected different results—e.g., instructing a subject, "Tell me what you see on this card" as opposed to, "Tell me everything you see on this card." The latter doesn't sound very different but can truly affect the nature of the verbal response.

The experimental manipulations should be spelled out in detail, with the qualifying assumption that overdoing the detail is inappropriate. We can assume that a reader perusing an experiment in the *Journal of the Experimental Analysis of Behavior* would know that a schedule of reinforcement reading "FR-10" would be a fixed ratio in which the animal was required to emit ten responses (bar presses, key pecks) before reinforcement was made available. A simple statement to this effect is all that may be necessary; the writer must expect some level of experience from readers of specific advanced journals.

In some studies there is a need to detail the *apparatus* or *equipment* that was used. Obviously, this detail is not needed when an investigator and subject have been on opposite sides of the table during an interview. (For example, "chairs were fixed-arm, leather-cushioned Grand Rapids inches above the floor.") But an experimental box, for example, should be named and described—including the manufacturer, model, and any unique features, all of which are relevant to assessing the experimental environment and for replicating it.

The *methods* section of the report should be brief but complete enough to explain exactly what was done, to whom, and in what kind of an environment.

Results. Up to this point the reader of your report has been told—with brilliant clarity, of course—why the study was initiated in the light of past research, the specific hypothesis or hypotheses to be tested, the subject population, and the experimental design by which the investigation will be conducted. Results are the factual products of all these elements.

The results should be as independent in presentation as an abstract, standing on their own without comment. The way results are presented depends upon the character of the data. Some data lend themselves readily to charts or tables; others may better appear as verbal accounts. Regardless of their form, the graphic presentation of results should be independent of the text, well labeled, and comprehensible so that the data speak for themselves. The written text should help the reader to connect the results shown in the tables and figures. You should try to avoid the redundancy that occurs when an author repeats in the written text the information already shown graphically.

I emphasize the factual nature of results because some investigators have a tendency to combine the Results and Discussion sections, presenting the results and at the same time commenting upon why they turned out the way they did. My own predilection is not to do it this way, because the reader should be able to read the findings of the study and come to conclusions of his own which may then be compared with the investigator's conclusions in the discussion section. At times, however, the combination of results and discussion may be acceptable. As David Shephard discusses this, they may be combined under four general conditions:

> a) when the results of a number of experiments are related closely enough to merit discussion together; b) when the results of each group of experiments require discussion as a set, perhaps in preparation for a general discussion later; c) when, otherwise, it would be necessary to repeat the results in the Discussion section; and d) when specific results of experiments or descriptions of clinical findings, in being reported at that point, lead to mention of generalizations. (113)

For the most part, however, it is better to state the results independently of discussion.

Shephard also sees some situations, similar to the results and discussion combination, that might occur in which you might wish to combine descriptions of methods and results

(113). These would include such circumstances as one experiment yielding results that lead to the conducting of another experiment. Again, on the whole, separating the sections is best.

Discussion. We have already covered the salient points of the discussion in the last section on results. Discussion should be the writer's opportunity to interpret the results achieved in the investigation. If the hypothesis was not supported by the experiment, the investigator has the chance to explain why this may be so. (Rarely does anyone explain why positive results were obtained!) Implications for the field, underscored by the contributions you have made in the light of the work of others, are part of the Discussion. Similarities and differences between the current work reported and results obtained by others form an important part of a discussion, and the writer should objectively evaluate them. The Discussion section is the sole opportunity for a bit of "editorializing" by the investigator. Based on the news that was offered in the Results section, the comments should be clear and logical extensions of the results of the study and the manner in which it was conducted.

References. In both the interpretative (review) and investigative (experimental, clinical) research reports, references are vital. Citations of previous work quoted should be listed as references, with detailed information so that the reader can identify the exact work cited. Sometimes it is also desirable to list books, articles, and journals that are relevant to the paper reported but have not been specifically cited in the body of the report. These citations should be listed separately, under "Bibliography" or "Suggestions for Further Reading" or a similar rubric. You will find such a listing at the back of this book.

Final Comments

In the brief compass of this chapter I have tried to present an overview of a highly complex task—writing the reports that tell the scientific community about the research that has been accomplished. It is obviously one of the most important functions a scientist has, for if research is not communicated it cannot serve to advance knowledge. I hope these general views and principles of research reporting have been helpful. They are intended to be not a "cookbook" to writing but simply a means of providing a greater familiarity with ways in which writing is organized. The major problem with most report writing is not in the performance of the task itself as much as in the organization to prepare for producing a report. You will undoubtedly have encountered resistance on your own part, from time to time and in varying degrees. You "don't feel" like writing a term paper and you might even delay it to the evening before it is due! Zounds! Organization is preparation through having your notes well collected (and readable), materials you will need readily available (from the obvious pencil and pad to index cards with references), and a sense of relaxation about setting something down on paper. Don't worry about writing a prize-winning paper; just set down ideas in order following the outline you have prepared. Relax; you will probably do a rewrite in any event. Writing can be enjoyable, if you allow it to be for yourself.

Appendices: Sample Research Forms

Introduction

In Chapter 9, when we spoke of ethical practices and procedures in conducting research, the topic of obtaining informed consent was covered as one of the more important aspects. It is now standard in all research involving human subjects to have potential research subjects sign a form consenting to take part in the research. The primary purpose of these consent forms is to make certain that the subject has a reasonably accurate idea of what the research is intended to accomplish and what his role is in it. Obviously, the forms will vary somewhat from one research setting to another but will generally fulfill the requirement of informing research subjects as to purpose and procedure.

Appendices A and B represent real documents used in my own research conducted at the Naval Medical Research Institute. The forms are specifically designed to cover the purposes and procedures of a particular research project, and are offered not as general forms but as examples of the type of background data and consent form needed for human research.

Appendix A is a series of questions which are directed toward meeting the Institute's requirements for the approval of proposed research. The answers to these questions are reviewed by the Committee for the Protection of Human Subjects (the committee responsible for the research in this case) and form the basis for a decision by the committee as to the ethical acceptability of the proposed research.

Appendix B is a consent form for the specific research project of which I am principal investigator, and therefore relates purposes and procedures only to that project. The subject, of course, is free to ask for other information to help in deciding whether or not to participate in the experiments.

APPENDIX A

Project Title: Physiological Performance and Human Engineering Evaluation of One-Atmosphere Diving Systems

Principal Investigator: A. J. Bachrach

Requirements for Review by the Committee for the Protection of Human Subjects

I. Please supply the following information and documentation:

A. What are the risks that may or may not be encountered by the subjects?

1. The normal risks of equipment failure are always a possibility, such as failure of the life-support system.
2. Subjects will be exposed to the normal risks associated with moderately strenuous exercise, and, as work continues, they may experience hyperthermic conditions.
3. There will also be the risks associated with immersion in water, which in the event of apparatus failure involving the system might result in drowning.
4. There is some discomfort from the application of ECG electrodes and the insertion of the rectal temperature probe, and there is risk of electric shock from monitoring apparatus.

B. What are the safeguards against these risks?

1. The work will be done by fully qualified U.S. Navy divers, using expertly engineered equipment, in protected, controlled water tanks under shallow conditions or controlled open sea dives. None of the dives will exceed a depth of 100 feet. The work will be done in an atmospheric diving suit, which is self-contained and has two redundant life-support systems (greater than 24 hours of support) acting as breathing reserve. The suit has weights that may be jettisoned at will. As a result, there will be no decompression from any dive, regardless of depth; decompression risks

180

are removed completely. For early research dives, this provides a safety factor 10 times the normal working exposure.

2. The amount of exercise required will be in a range considered to be something more than moderate by the subject. Deep body temperature will be continuously monitored and a noticeable rise beyond predetermined safe levels will cause an immediate abort of the experiment. Heart rate will be continuously monitored and full resuscitative measures will be immediately available.

   Qualified diving supervisors and medically trained personnel will be in continuous attendance, with close medical and physiological observation and monitoring throughout the experiments.

3. Safety divers and tenders will be available at all times that a subject is immersed.

4. The shock potential of the ECG has been eliminated by the introduction of an optical isolator in the transmitting package.

C. *Have the elements of informed consent been satisfied? The consent will be obtained in writing. Attach a copy of the consent form.*

A copy of the consent form is appended.

D. *Are the procedures established and accepted nationally and locally and/or for the patients' benefit?*

The procedures established are nationally and locally accepted.

APPENDIX B

**Consent to Voluntarily Participate
in a Research Development Test or
Evaluation (RDT&E) Procedure**

1.   I hereby volunteer to participate as a subject in a research program being conducted under the work unit title "Physiological Performance and Human Engineering Evaluation of One-Atmosphere Diving Systems."

2.   I understand that the following procedures will be employed in this study: I will be performing specially developed underwater performance tasks, related to tasks a Navy diver would ordinarily be performing, such as placing and securing patches on equipment to secure them as water-tight, connecting bolts to equipment to assemble different pieces of apparatus, and torquing down bolts, which will be accomplished while I am operating a 1 ATA diving system from inside. I understand that in addition to work measurements and procedures, physiological measures will be taken in a number of different situations. These conditions are: electrodes for heart rates (electrocardiograms), rectal temperature probes to obtain body temperature, respiration rate to measure breathing. Urine samples will be taken at time of pre- and post-experiments. These are standard physiological measures accomplished under proper supervision. The depths will average 20 feet and at no time in this experimental phase be deeper than 100 feet.

3.   The work will be done using a tested one-atmosphere diving system in protected tanks and shallow conditions under approved Navy diving procedures.

4.   I understand that the information derived from this study will ultimately provide a basis for improved development of underwater task performance that will benefit dive planning, dive efficiency and safety.

5.   I understand that I am free at any time to make any inquiries concerning the procedures employed in this study and the investigators will freely respond to these inquiries.

6.   I understand that I can withdraw from the study or freely omit procedures without reproach and without jeopardizing my status at any time that I wish.

7.   I have read both this consent form and the form approved for this study by the NMRI Committee for the Protection of Human Subjects.

8.   All personal information on individual subjects will remain confidential in accordance with the Privacy Act.

Date: _____   *Signed:* _____

                                            _____
                                            (typed name, rate, rank or grade)

Witnessed: _____   *Date of Birth:* _____

                                            Approved: _____

Bibliography

1. Aaronson, S. Style in scientific writing. *Current Contents,* 1977, *20* (2), 6–15.
2. American Psychological Association. *Principles for the care and use of animals.* (Official policy statement of the Committee on Animal Research and Experimentation.) Washington, D.C.: American Psychological Association, 1979.
3. Arnold, M. *Emotions and personality* (Vol. 1.) New York: Columbia University Press, 1960, p. 143.
4. Aserinsky, E., & Kleitman, N. Regularly occurring periods of eye motility and concomitant phenomena during sleep. *Science,* 1953, *118,* 273–274.
5. Asimov, I. *The intelligent man's guide to science* (Vol. 1: *The physical sciences).* New York: Basic Books, 1960, p. 290.
6. Bachrach, A.J. The ethics of tachistoscopy. *Bulletin of the Atomic Scientists,* 1959, *5,* 12–215.
7. *Ibid.,* p. 214.
8. Bachrach, A. J. An experimental approach to superstitious behavior. *Journal of American Folklore,* 1962, *75,* 1–9.
9. Bachrach, A. J. Learning theory. In A. M. Freedman, H. I. Kaplan, & B. J. Sadock (Eds.), *Comprehensive textbook of psychiatry* (Vol. 3). Baltimore: Williams & Wilkins, 1980.
10. Bachrach, A. J. Psychophysiological factors in diving. *Weekly Update: Hyperbaric and Undersea Medicine.* Princeton, N.J.: Biomedia, Inc., 1978, *1* (29).
11. Bachrach, A. J. (Ed.). *Experimental foundations of clinical psychology.* New York: Basic Books, 1962.
12. Bachrach, A. J., Banghart, F. W., & Pattishall, E. G. Comments on the diagnostician as computer. *Neuropsychiatry,* 1960, *6,* 32.
13. Bachrach, A. J., & Pattishall, E. G. An experiment in universal

and personal validation. *Psychiatry: Journal for the Study of Interpersonal Processes,* 1960, *23,* 267–270.

14. Baldwin, A. L. The study of child behavior and development. In P. H. Mussen (Ed.), *Handbook of research methods in child development.* New York: Wiley, 1960, pp. 3–35.

15. Barber, B. Resistance by scientists to scientific discovery. *Science,* 1961, *134,* 596–602.

16. *Ibid.,* pp. 4–5.

17. *Ibid.,* pp. 6–7.

18. Barber, B., & Fox, R. C. The case of the floppy-eared rabbits: An instance of serendipity gained and serendipity lost. *American Journal of Sociology,* 1958, *54,* 128–136.

19. *Ibid.,* p. 130.

20. *Ibid.,* p. 131.

21. *Ibid.,* p. 132.

22. *Ibid.,* p. 134.

23. *Ibid.,* p. 135.

24. Bellanca, J. J. Asbestos-related diseases. *U.S. Navy Medicine,* 1979, *70* (5), 18–19.

25. Berg, I. A. The use of human subjects in psychological research. *American Psychologist,* 1954, *9,* 108–111.

26. Bondi, H. Why scientists talk. In John Wolfenden, *The language of science: A survey of techniques of communication.* New York: Basic Books, 1963, pp. 19–38.

27. *Ibid.,* p. 25.

28. *Ibid.,* p. 25.

29. Brady, J. V. Emotional behavior. In J. Field, V. E. Hall, & H. W. Magoun (Eds.), *Handbook of Physiology.* (Vol. 3, Sec. 1: *Neurophysiology*). Bethesda, Md.: American Physiological Society, 1959, p. 1529.

30. Bridgman, P. W. *The intelligent individual and society.* New York: Macmillan, 1938.

31. Bronowski, J. *The common sense of science.* Cambridge: Harvard University Press, 1953, p. 70.

32. *Ibid.,* p. 130.

33. *Ibid.,* p. 131.

34. Bronowski, J. *Science and human values.* New York: Harper & Row, 1959, pp. 66–67.

35. *Ibid.,* p. 80.

36. *Ibid.,* pp. 77–78.

37. *Ibid.*, pp. 90-91.
38. Brunswik, E. The conceptual framework of psychology. *International Encyclopedia of Unified Sciences,* 1952, *6,* 659-751.
39. Bryson, B. Fractured English. *Aloft,* May-June 1979, pp. 68-72.
40. Bugental, J. F. T. *The search for authenticity.* New York: Holt, Rinehart & Winston, 1965, pp. 13-14.
41. Bustad, L. K. The experimental subject—a choice not an echo. *Perspectives in Biology and Medicine,* 1970, *14,* 1-10.
42. Canadian Cooperative Study Group. A randomized trial of aspirin and sulfinpyrazone in threatened stroke. *New England Journal of Medicine,* 1978, *299,* 53-59.
43. The Canadian Medical Association statement on death, November 1968. In Association News, *Canadian Medical Association Journal,* December 28, 1968, pp. 1266-1267.
44. Cannon, W. B. *The way of an investigator.* New York: Norton, 1945.
45. Chase, S. *The tyranny of words.* New York: Harcourt, Brace, 1938, p. 21
46. *Ibid.*
47. *Ibid.*, p. 380.
48. Cohen, R. S., quoted in M. W. Wartofsky, *Conceptual foundations of scientific thought: An introduction to the philosophy of science.* New York: Macmillan, 1968, p. 414.
49. Coronary Drug Project Research Group. The coronary drug project aspirin study: Implications for clinical care. *Primary Care,* 1978, *5* (1), 91-95.
50. Cronbach, L. J. The two disciplines of scientific psychology. *American Psychologist,* 1957, *12,* 671-684.
51. Curtis, P. New debate over experimenting with animals. *New York Times,* December 31, 1978. Condensed as "The case against animal experiments," *Reader's Digest,* February 1980, pp. 181-186.
52. Davis, K. Mental hygiene and the class structure. In A. Rose (Ed.), *Mental health and mental disorder.* New York: W.W. Norton, 1955, p. 580
53. Davis, R. C. Physical psychology. *Psychological Review,* 1953, *60,* 7-14.
54. Day, R. A. *How to write and publish a scientific paper.* Philadelphia: ISC Press, 1979.
55. de Ford, C. S., quoted in M. Gardner, *Fads and fallacies in the name of science.* New York: Dover, 1957, p. 12.

56. DeVore, I., & Washburn, S. I. Baboon ecology and human evolution. In F. C. Howell & F. Bouliere (Eds.), *African ecology and human evolution*. Viking Fund Publications in Anthropology, No. 36. New York: Wenner Gren Foundation, 1963, pp. 335–367.

57. Diaconis, P. Statistical problems in ESP research. *Science*, 1978, *201*, 131–136.

58. *Diagnostic and statistical manual of mental disorders*. Washington, D.C.: American Psychiatric Association, 1952.

59. Dreher, J., & Bachrach, A. J. Power spectral density: A method for the rhythm analysis of disordered speech. In D. V. Siva Sankar (Ed.), *Schizophrenia: Current concepts and research*. Hicksville, N.Y.: PJD Publications, 1969.

60. English, O. S., & Finch, S. M. *Introduction to psychiatry*. New York: Norton, 1954.

61. *Ethical Standards of Psychologists* (Rev. ed.). Washington, D.C.: American Psychological Association, 1977, pp. 6–7.

62. Fagin, L. *More than you want to know about scientific writing*. Mimeographed, not dated.

63. Feigl, H. Operationism and scientific method. *Psychological Review*, 1945, *52*, 250–259.

64. Fleming, A. On the antibacterial action of cultures of a penicillium, with special reference to their use in the isolation of *B. Influenze. British Journal of Experimental Pathology*, 1929, *10*, 226–236.

65. Forer, B. R. The fallacy of personal validation: A classroom demonstration of gullibility. *Journal of Abnormal and Social Psychology*, 1949, *14*, 118–123.

66. Fox, R. C. *Experiment perilous: Physicians and patients facing the unknown*. Glencoe, Ill.: The Free Press, 1959.

67. Freud, A. *The ego and the mechanisms of defense*. New York: International Universities, 1948, p. 43.

68. Gardner, M. Dermo-optical perception: A peek down the nose. *Science*, 1966, *151*, 654–657.

69. Gardner, M. *Fads and fallacies in the name of science*. New York: Dover, 1957, p. 30.

70. *Ibid.*, p. 11.

71. Graves, R., & Hodge, A. *The reader over your shoulder* (2nd ed.). New York: Vintage Books, 1971, p. 15.

72. Gray, B. H., Cooke, R. A., & Tannenbaum, A. S. Research involving human subjects. *Science*, 1978, *201*, 1094–1101.

73. Greenspoon, J. Private experience revisited. *Psychological Record*, 1961, *11*, 373–381.

74. Gustavson, C. R., Garcia, J., Hankins, W. G., & Rusiniak, K. W. Coyote predation control by aversive conditioning. *Science*, 1974, *184*, 581–583.

75. Gustavson, C. R., Kelly, D. J. Sweeney, M., and Garcia, J. Prey-lithium aversions: I. Coyotes and wolves. *Behavioral Biology*, 1976, *17*, 61–72.

76. Hall, C. S. *The meaning of dreams*. McGraw-Hill, 1966.

77. Hecht, S. *Exploring the atom*. New York: Viking, 1948, p. 7.

78. Hefferline, R. F., Keenan, B., & Harford, R. A. Escape and avoidance conditioning in human subjects without their observation of the response. *Science*, 1959, *130*, 1338–1339.

79. Hobson, J. A., Spagna, T., & Malenka, R. Ethology of sleep studies with time-lapse photography: Postural immobility and sleep-cycle in humans. *Science*, 1978, *201* (29), 1251–1253.

80. Hoiberg, A. Women in the Navy: Morale and attrition. *Armed Forces and Society*, 1978, *4* (4), 659–671.

81. Hull, C. L. Hypothetico-deductive method of theory construction. In L. Stolurow (Ed.), *Readings in learning*. Englewood Cliffs, N.J.: Prentice-Hall, 1953, pp. 9–30.

82. Ivan, L. T. Irreversible brain damage and related problems: Pronouncement of death. *Journal of the American Geriatrics Society*, 1970, *18*, 816–822.

83. Jourard, S. M. *Disclosing man to himself*. Princeton, N.J.: Van Nostrand, 1968.

84. Kelman, H. C. The human use of human subjects: The problem of deception in social-psychological experiments. Paper delivered at the seventy-third annual convention of the American Psychological Association, Chicago, 1965.

85. Kimmel, A. J. Ethics and human subjects: Research, a delicate balance. *American Psychologist*, July 1979, pp. 633–635.

86. Kluckhohn, C. Culture and behavior. In G. Lindzey (Ed.), *Handbook of social psychology* (Vol. 2). Cambridge: Addison-Wesley, 1954, p. 938.

87. Kluckhohn, F. R. Dominant and substitute profiles of cultural orientations: Their significance for the analysis of social stratification. *Social Forces*, 1950, *28*, 376–393.

88. Kuhn, T. *The structure of scientific revolutions*. Chicago: University of Chicago, 1962.

89. *Ibid.,* p. 10.

90. *Ibid.,* p. 159.

91. *Ibid.,* p. 166.

92. Leavitt, E. M. *Animals and their legal rights.* Washington, D.C.: Animal Welfare Institute, 1978.

93. Levy, C. M., & Brackbill, Y. Informed consent: Getting the message across to kids. *APA Monitor,* 1979, *10* (3), 3.

94. Lief, H. I. Sensory association in the selection of phobic objects. *Psychiatry,* 1955, *18,* 331.

95. Lipton, J. *An exaltation of larks: or the venereal game.* New York: Penguin Books, 1977, p. 3.

96. Malinowksi, B. Magic, science and religion. In J. Needham (Ed.), *Science, religion and reality.* New York: Macmillan, 1925, p. 32.

97. Margenau, H. Philosophical problems in physics. In C. W. Churchman & P. Ratoosh (Eds.), *Measurement: Definition and theories.* New York: Wiley, 1959, pp. 167ff.

98. Marx, M. H. The general nature of theory construction. In M. H. Marx (Ed.), *Psychological theory.* New York: Macmillan, 1950, pp. 7–8.

99. Nelson, G. Interview. In S. Rosner & L. E. Abt (Eds.), *The creative experience.* New York: Grossman, 1970, pp. 251–268.

100. Norton, A. R. Terrorists, atoms and the future: Understanding the threat. *Naval War College Review,* May/June 1979, pp. 30–50.

101. O'Brien, J. R. Effects of salicylates on human platelets. *Lancet,* 1968, *1,* 779–783.

102. Orwell, G. Politics and the English language. In G. Orwell, *Shooting an elephant and other essays.* New York: Harcourt, Brace, 1950.

103. The out-of-it-alphabet. *Esquire,* August 1979, pp. 70–71.

104. Packard, V. *The people shapers.* Boston: Little, Brown, 1977.

105. Pauli, D. C., & Clapper, G. P. (Eds.). *Project Sealab report: An experimental 45-day undersea saturation dive at 205 feet.* Washington, D.C.: Office of Naval Research, 1967.

106. Polya, G. *How to solve it: A new aspect of mathematical method* (2nd ed.). Garden City, N.J.: Doubleday, 1957.

107. Quine, W. *Truth by convention.* In Otis H. Lee (Ed.), *Philosophical essays for Alfred North Whitehead.* New York: Longmans Greens, 1946.

108. Rapoport, A. *Operational philosophy*. New York: Harper and Bros., 1954, p. 74.

109. Rapoport, A. What is semantics? *American Scientist*, 1952, *40*, 123–135.

110. Reichenbach, H. *Experience and prediction*. Chicago: University of Chicago Press, 1938.

111. Renan, E. *The future of science*, 1848.

112. Schultz, D. P. The human subject in psychological research. *Psychological Bulletin*, 1969, *72*, 214–228.

113. Shephard, D. A. E. Parts of the scientific paper (Pt. 2). *Medical Communications*, 1975, *3* (4).

114. Shilling, C. W., & Werts, M. F. *Underwater medicine and related sciences* (Vol. 3: *A guide to the literature*). Bethesda, Md.: Undersea Medical Society, 1977.

115. Sidman, M. *Tactics of scientific research*. New York: Basic Books, 1960, p. 15.

116. *Ibid.*, p. 9.

117. *Ibid.*, p. 9.

118. *Ibid.*, p. 17.

119. *Ibid.*, p. 27.

120. *Ibid.*, p. 27.

121. *Ibid.*, p. 28.

122. Sidman, M. Verplanck's analysis of Skinner. *Contemporary Psychology*, 1956, *1*, 8.

123. Skinner, B. F. A case history in scientific method. In B. F. Skinner, *Cumulative Record*. New York: Macmillan, 1956, p. 81.

124. Skinner, B. F. *Science and human behavior*. New York: Macmillan, 1953, p. 13.

125. *Ibid.*, p. 12.

126. *Ibid.*, p. 12.

127. *Ibid.*, p. 13.

128. *Ibid.*, p. 38–39.

129. Skinner, B. F. "Superstition" in the pigeon. *Journal of Experimental Psychology*, 1948, *38*, 168–172.

130. Skinner, B. F. *Verbal behavior*. New York: Appleton-Century-Crofts, 1957, pp. 8–9.

131. Skinner, B. F., & Morse, W. H. A second type of "superstition" in the pigeon. *American Journal of Psychology*, 1957, *70*, 308–311.

132. Sorensen, T. C. *Kennedy*. New York: Harper & Row, 1965.

133. Stein, J. The bioethicists: Facing matters of life and death. *Smithsonian,* January 1979, 107–115.

134. Stevens, C. Experiments on animals in the United States and developing substitutes. *Information Report, Animal Welfare Institute,* 1978, *27* (3).

135. Stevens, S. S. Psychology and the science of science. *Psychological Bulletin,* 1939, *36.*

136. Stevenson, I. P. *The evidence for survival from claimed memories of former incarnations.* Surrey, England: M. C. Peto, 1961.

137. Stone, L. J. Recent developments in diagnostic testing of children. In R. E. Harris, *Recent advances in diagnostic psychological testing.* Springfield, Mass.: Thomas, 1950, pp. 82–83.

138. Szent–Gyorgyi, A. Looking back. *Perspectives in Biology and Medicine,* 1971, *13,* 1.

139. Taton, R. *[Reason and chance in scientific discovery]* (A. J. Pomerans, trans. from French). New York: Philosophical Library, 1957.

140. Underwood, B. J. *Psychological research.* New York: Appleton-Century-Crofts, 1957, p. 19.

141. Van Lawick–Goodall, J. *In the shadow of man.* Boston: Houghton-Mifflin, 1971.

142. Visscher, M. B. Animal rights and alternative methods. *The Pharos,* Fall 1979, 11–19.

143. Walter, W. G. *The living brain.* New York: Norton, 1953, p. 33.

144. Wartofsky, M. W. *Conceptual foundations of scientific thought: An introduction to the philosophy of science.* New York: Macmillan, 1968.

145. Weber, M. *The methodology of the social sciences.* Glencoe, Ill.: The Free Press, 1949.

146. Weis, H. J., & Aledort, L. M. Impaired platelet-connective-tissue reaction in man after aspirin ingestion. *Lancet,* 1967, *2,* 495–497.

147. Wenger, M., Jones, F. N., & Jones, M. H. *Physiological psychology.* New York: Holt, Rinehart and Winston, 1956.

148. Wolpe, J. The experimental foundation of some new therapeutic methods. In A. J. Bachrach (Ed.), *Experimental foundations of clinical psychology.* New York: Basic Books, 1962, pp. 554–575.

149. Wolpe, J. *Psychotherapy by reciprocal inhibition.* Palo Alto: Stanford University Press, 1958.

150. *Women at the Naval Academy: The first year of integration*

(NPRDC Report TR-78-12). Naval Personnel Research & Development Center, 1978.

151.   *Women content in units: Force development test (MAX WAC).* U.S. Army Research Institute Report, October 3, 1977.

152.   Young, J. Z. *Doubt and certainty in science.* Oxford: Clarendon Press, 1951, pp. 1-2.

153.   Zuckerman, S. The breeding season of mammals in captivity. *Proceedings of the Zoological Society of London,* 1953, *122,* 827-950.

Suggestions for Further Reading

In addition to references cited in the text, there are several volumes which illustrate the ways in which investigators work and the way science as a creative endeavor develops. These are:

Glasser, Ronald J. *The body is the hero*. New York: Random House, 1976.

Kaplan, Abraham. *The conduct of inquiry*. San Francisco: Chandler, 1964.

Medawar, Peter B. *Advice to a young scientist*. New York: Harper & Row, 1979.

Popper, Karl A. *Conjectures and refutations*. London: Routledge & Kegan Paul, 1972.

Popper, Karl A. *The logic of scientific discovery*. London: Hutchinson, 1972.

Trefil, James. *Physics as a liberal art*. New York: Pergamon, 1978.

An excellent source of information on scientific writing is:

Woodford, F. Peter. *Scientific writing for graduate students: A manual on the teaching of scientific writing*. Washington, D.C.: Council of Biology Editors, 1976.

and for the use of graphics and illustrations:

MacGregor, A. J. *Graphics simplified*. Toronto: University of Toronto Press, 1979.

Index